T0318954

Cambridge Elements ≡

Elements in Child Development
edited by
Marc H. Bornstein
National Institute of Child Health and Human Development, Bethesda
Institute for Fiscal Studies, London
UNICEF, New York City

THE SCIENCE OF CHILDREN'S RELIGIOUS AND SPIRITUAL DEVELOPMENT

Annette Mahoney
Bowling Green State University

CAMBRIDGE
UNIVERSITY PRESS

CAMBRIDGE
UNIVERSITY PRESS

University Printing House, Cambridge CB2 8BS, United Kingdom

One Liberty Plaza, 20th Floor, New York, NY 10006, USA

477 Williamstown Road, Port Melbourne, VIC 3207, Australia

314–321, 3rd Floor, Plot 3, Splendor Forum, Jasola District Centre,
New Delhi – 110025, India

103 Penang Road, #05–06/07, Visioncrest Commercial, Singapore 238467

Cambridge University Press is part of the University of Cambridge.

It furthers the University's mission by disseminating knowledge in the pursuit of education, learning, and research at the highest international levels of excellence.

www.cambridge.org
Information on this title: www.cambridge.org/9781108812771
DOI: 10.1017/9781108874342

First published 2021

A catalogue record for this publication is available from the British Library.

ISBN 978-1-108-81277-1 Paperback
ISSN 2632-9948 (online)
ISSN 2632-993X (print)

The Science of Children's Religious and Spiritual Development

Elements in Child Development

DOI: 10.1017/9781108874342
First published online: July 2021

Annette Mahoney
Bowling Green State University
Author for correspondence: Annette Mahoney, amahone@bgsu.edu

Abstract: This Element provides a comprehensive yet concise account of scientific research on children's religious and spiritual (RS) development up to age 12. After providing a historical sketch of definitional issues in the science of RS, the first section reviews basic descriptive information on children's RS development as well as wholistic theoretical models and measures of children's RS development. The second section covers evidence about links of child and parental RS to children's psychosocial adjustment and highlights the need for more research that discriminates specific positive and negative manifestations of RS for children's development. The third section summarizes evidence about the robust influence of parents on their children's RS development and parents' perceptions of their role in this process. The fourth section focuses on cognitive-developmental research on children's cognitions about God/deities and prayer. The Element concludes with a synopsis of key themes and challenges that researchers face to advance the science of children's RS development.

Keywords: religion, spirituality, children, faith development, parenting

ISBNs: 9781108812771 (PB), 9781108874342 (OC)
ISSNs: 2632-9948 (online), 2632-993X (print)

Contents

Introduction

According to a 2014 Pew US national survey, teaching children to be responsible emerged as the top goal that parents endorsed out of twelve options, with 94 percent saying this child-rearing outcome was "especially important." Instilling the ability to work hard was the second most endorsed goal (92 percent), followed by rearing children to be helpful (86 percent), well-mannered (86 percent), and independent (79 percent). In short, almost all US parents wanted their children to become good (i.e., prosocial) people per these criteria. Furthermore, these top five parenting goals did not vary according to parents' religious affiliation or lack thereof. Echoing centuries of exhortation from religious leaders, however, a growing chorus of social scientists urge parents to facilitate their children's religious and spiritual (RS)[1] development to help them become good as well as happy people (e.g., Miller, 2015; Roehlkepartain, 2014). This focus on families makes sense given that parents are the biggest influence in their children's RS development, at least based on scientific data drawn largely from Western societies (Bengtson, Putney, & Harris, 2013; 2013; Smith & Adamczyk, 2021). For example, according to a 2019 US national survey, teens who say they attend religious services at least monthly (44 percent) have parents who do the same (43 percent; Pew, 2020). Such data exemplify a long-standing emphasis in human societies on the transmission of RS beliefs and practices from families to offspring as an important road for children to traverse to be well-adjusted across the lifespan (Bengston et al., 2013; Smith & Adamczyk, 2021).

Most parents living with children around the world also say that religion is an important dimension of their family life. In a 2008 cross-cultural survey spanning China, Colombia, Italy, Jordan, Kenya, the Philippines, Sweden, Thailand, and the United States, mothers and fathers strongly agreed, on average, that religion influences their parenting and is important in their lives (Bornstein et al., 2017). Also, in the United States, 79 percent of married mothers, 77 percent of single mothers, and 68 percent of cohabiting mothers reported that religion is "somewhat" or "very important" to their daily life based on 2011–13 national surveys (Mahoney, Larrid, Payne, & Manning, 2015). In short, many millions of families across the globe likely view bestowing their children with RS resources as important to supporting their children's development.

---

[1] The abbreviation RS is used throughout this Element to denote Religious/Religion (R) and Spiritual/Spirituality (S) because these complex, multifaceted domains overlap conceptually and empirically. Refer to the section "Defining of Religious/Religion and Spiritual/Spirituality" for elaboration.

Despite these statistics, rising secularization in many regions of the world suggests dwindling success by adults to foster children's RS development (Voas & Chaves, 2016). For example, as of 2019, US teens are far less likely to pray daily than their parents (27 percent of teens versus 48 percent of parents), say that religion is very important in their lives (24 percent versus 43 percent), and believe in God with absolute certainty (40 percent versus 63 percent; Pew, 2020). Annual US surveys between 1974 and 2014 also document marked declines in young adults (ages 18–29) labeling themselves as being a spiritual or a religious person, viewing the Bible as literally true, and having confidence in organized religion (Twenge, Sherman, Exline, & Grubbs, 2016). Although as of 2017, 83 percent of US young adults still report believing in God or a higher power or spiritual force, only 43 percent endorse belief in God as described in the Bible (Pew, 2018a). Data on young adults in other Western democratic countries that have historically been predominantly Christian (e.g., Europe, Canada, Australia) also show marked declines in personal (e.g., prayer) and public participation in religion (e.g., religious attendance; Pew, 2018b). Adolescents' participation in organized religious groups across most other countries has also declined relative to older generations, although less sharply (Pew, 2018b). Simultaneously, Western societies have witnessed a rapid rise in the young adults identifying as atheist or agnostic and rejecting any religious affiliation (Thiessen & Wilkins-Laflamme, 2020).

Overall, these shifting patterns in the intergenerational transmission of RS hint at a growing polarization across the globe about which children may gain the benefits and be exposed to the risks of RS becoming a core part of their identity. Furthermore, potentially escalating divisions could emerge about whether and how to foster a child's (non)faith development between generations and across societies. Given these tensions, it is perhaps all the more important to know what science currently does and does not tell us about the nature and implications of children's RS development up to age twelve. This Element addresses this topic. More specifically, this Element aims to help readers understand what social scientists know about children's RS development. The primary audience for this Element consists of social scientists who are curious about this topic, a largely neglected subject within academia. As of 2017, for example, Richert, Boyatzis and King (2017) estimated that fewer than 0.5 percent of developmental science has focused on RS development for youth of any age, with the overwhelming emphasis on adolescents (ages 13–20) rather than children (ages 3–12). Nevertheless, many researchers as well as parents, educators, and helping professionals may be eager to learn what we know empirically about children's RS development.

This Element is structured as follows to provide readers with a comprehensive but concise account of the available scientifically based information about children's RS development. I start with a historical sketch of the difficulties in defining the domains of religion and spirituality and the four loosely organized communities of social scientists who appear to have most often grappled with children's RS development. These groups include (1) RS educators and scholars, (2) social scientists especially interested in RS and children's well-being, (3) sociologists especially interested in intergenerational transmission of religious traditions' affiliation, beliefs, and practices, and (4) social and cognitive-developmental scientists especially interested in children's supernatural cognitions. The bulk of this Element is then devoted to four major sections about children's RS development as follows.

The first major section addresses ways that social scientists rooted in Western cultures have attempted to define and measure children's RS development. This section highlights the lack of consensus on these two most basic issues and reveals remarkable disconnects between abstract theoretical definitions of children's RS development versus the nitty-gritty empirical questionnaires used to investigate wholistic models of children's RS development. Notably, although wholistic models avoid theistic terminology, nearly all of the corresponding quantitative studies with children as participants ask the children about their thoughts or feelings toward "God." In the second major section, I elaborate on emerging and intriguing empirical research on the potential benefits and risks of children's RS for their psychosocial adjustment. In addition, I summarize evidence of parents' RS functioning shaping their parenting practices in positive and negative ways that contribute to children's psychological functioning.

The third and fourth major sections of the Element shift toward factors thought to shape the development of children's RS thoughts and feelings rather than possible outcomes tied to their RS functioning. Ideally, related scientific evidence would fit neatly into Bronferbrenner's (Bronfenbrenner & Morris, 2006) familiar bioecological model of human development that highlights biological, child, family, peers, school, and local religious communities, as well as broader cultural contexts that reciprocally and interactively shape children's development over time. The reality, however, is that the bulk of this literature addresses (1) the intergenerational transmission from parents to youth of an affiliation with a major world religion and associated beliefs and practices and (2) children's cognitions about supernatural phenomena during early and middle childhood. Hence, the third major section summarizes quantitative evidence about the influence of parents on their children's RS (non) socialization. The fourth major section focuses on a complex body of quantitative surveys and experimental laboratory research on children's cognitions about God/deities and prayer, noting the virtual absence of research on children's views of evil supernatural powers. The Element concludes with a fifth section on the challenges that researchers face to advance the science of children's RS development.

Historical Sketch of Science on Children's Religious and Spiritual (RS) Development

This portion of the Element provides a primer on conceptual complexities in defining Religious/Religion (R) versus Spiritual/Spirituality (S) within social science literature. Understanding these issues is necessary to appreciate the nature of the empirical findings delineated throughout this Element. I also offer a historical sketch of four loosely organized groups of social scientists who have explored the topic of children's RS development.

Defining of Religious/Religion and Spiritual/Spirituality

Perhaps the most basic point to understand about children's RS development is that a clear consensus does not exist among social scientists about the overarching definitions and boundaries between the multifaceted domains of being Religious/Religion (R) versus being Spiritual/Spirituality (S) when studying people across the lifespan (Hill & Edwards, 2013; Kapuscinski & Masters, 2010; Oman, 2013). In general, being R is portrayed within sociological and psychological literature as public engagement in a given organized sociocultural-historical religious tradition; adherence to theologically orthodox beliefs, dogmas, or rituals, especially in relationship to supernatural entities; and external pressure to conform to social norms promoted by a religious group (Pargament, Mahoney, Exline, Jones, & Shafranske, 2013). One widely used definition of religion in the social science literature, for instance, has been:

> an organized system of beliefs, practices, rituals, and symbols that serve (a) to facilitate individuals' closeness to the sacred or transcendent other (i.e., God, higher power, ultimate truth) and (b) to bring about an understanding of an individual's relationship and responsibility to others living together in community (Koenig, McCullough, & Larson, 2001, p.18).

Along these lines, attendance at worship services and endorsement of conservative Christian beliefs (e.g., literalist interpretations of the Bible) have typically been labeled as being "religious," "religiousness," or "religiosity." Notably, some scholars have recommended that the term "religion" per se be reserved for scholarship about organized religious institutions that promote particular theological worldviews and practices whereas the term "religiousness" be used for social science investigations into the characteristics of people who report on their experiences, cognitions, or behaviors consistent with one or more religion's teachings (Paloutzian & Park, 2021). This semantic distinction encourages social scientists not to portray themselves as experts on the history, theology, or veracity of truth claims promoted by various world religions, leaving such work to philosophers, theologians, and/or religious studies scholars.

Within the social science literature, the domain of being spiritual tends to be framed as a personal search for a connection to divine entities or supernatural phenomena; a private quest for enlightenment or virtues; and/or internal motivation to seek out meaning, purpose, and self-transcendence within or outside of the self or organized religion groups. Koenig et al. (2001), for example, defined spirituality as "a personal quest for understanding answers to ultimate questions about life, about meaning, and about relationship to the sacred or transcendent, which may (or may not) lead to or arise from the development of religious rituals and the formation of community" (p. 18). Importantly, in an effort to be maximally inclusive and based on the assumption that all humans are inherently "spiritual" by nature, some social scientists argue that the boundaries of spirituality encompass children organizing their sense of meaning and purpose around anything perceived as "larger than the self" (Roehlkepartain, 2014). From this vantage point, self-transcendence as a prototypical element of spirituality does not need to involve supernatural entities or experiences (Miller, 2015; Roehlkepartain, 2014). Likewise, spirituality need not involve organized religious traditions. To illustrate, Boyatzis (2012, p. 153) argued that "children are spiritual beings first and then are acculturated (or not) in a religious tradition that channels intuitive spirituality into particular expressions (rituals, creeds, etc.) that have been passed through the faith tradition."

Given the expansive definitions of S used in social science literature, a persistent and elusive definitional problem is what makes either R or S substantively distinctive from any other domain of life (Kapuscinski & Masters, 2010; Pargament et al., 2013). The first major section of this Element that covers wholistic models of children's spiritual well-being will vividly illustrate this issue and the conclusions section of this Element will revisit the difficulties of polarizing R versus S in research on children's RS development given available theoretical and empirical knowledge. In the meantime, I use the abbreviation RS throughout this Element to refer to research on children's RS development because, when models and measures are closely examined, findings seem to converge on one construct that has been uniquely and consistently studied for children – namely, their perceptions of God. For additional cogent elaborations on defining R and S, see Nelson (2009) and Oman (2013). A brief sketch of four loosely organized communities of scholars and social scientists who have most often grappled with children's RS development is instructive to begin to understand the sometimes bewildering language used in scientific literature on children's RS development.

Four Loosely Organized Communities of Scholars and Social Scientists

Although the domain of RS was at the forefront of work by early pioneers in psychiatry (e.g., Sigmund Freud, Carl Jung), psychology (e.g., William James), and sociology (e.g., Emile Durkheim), social scientists devoted to the field of child development in the twentieth century seemed to have generally been disinterested in the topic (Boyatzis, 2013; Holden & Williamson, 2014). The major exception was Fowler (1981), who in the late 1970s proposed an influential stage model of RS development that integrated concepts from Piaget's theory of cognitive development, Kohlberg's theory of moral development, and Erikson's theory of psychosocial development. Fowler proposed that humans pass through three primitive stages of faith development from birth to adolescence (i.e., primal faith, intuitive-projective faith, mythical-literal faith) and that RS primarily emerges as important after the onset of the cognitive stage of formal operations in adolescence and into adulthood. Fowler viewed mature cognitive skills as necessary for individuals to comprehend RS issues and make upward progress across adulthood through what Fowler viewed as increasingly sophisticated stages of faith. Fowler's assumptions perhaps helped to dampen interest by mainstream developmental scientists in investigating children's RS. However, the following four communities of scholars and social scientists have been steadily increasing the body of empirical research focused on children's RS over the past two to three decades.

Religious educators and scholars. In opposition to Fowler's assumptions, scholars with a strong interest in children's RS education were among the first to interview young children to solicit their stories and artwork (e.g., drawings, paintings) about their experiences of God, religious teachings, scriptures, and interconnectedness with nature and other people. Leading figures include psychiatrist Coles (1990), who wrote an influential narrative account of children's spirituality rooted in psychoanalytic theory, and Hay and Nye (1998), who interviewed thirty-eight 6- to 11-year-old children from the United Kingdom, most of whom (74 percent) were not affiliated with a religious tradition. Based on these and other studies (Mata-McMahon, 2016), scholars in this area encouraged religious educators to avoid didactic and rote instruction of orthodox religious belief or practices, and instead nondirectively explore children's sense of in-the-moment flow (awareness sensing), wonder and awe (mystery sensing), and feelings of ultimate goodness and meaning underlying being alive (value sensing). Mata-McMahon (2016) has written an analysis of this largely ethnographic and qualitative body of literature. A major journal that has published work by these scholars is the *International Journal of Children's Spirituality.*

Social scientists interested in children's RS and psychosocial well-being. Beginning in the 1990s, social scientists started to formulate conceptual models and quantitative assessment tools to capture wholistic portrayals of children's RS well-being. Drawing on the qualitative work mentioned earlier, this research emphasizes the language of "children's spirituality," although most measures assess children's understanding of God and/or activities encouraged by organized religious groups (e.g., prayer). Fisher (1998), in particular, spearheaded such work by interviewing teachers from Australia about their ideas of the best ways to facilitate children's RS formation. Fisher then developed separate structured tools to assess adolescents' and children's "spiritual well-being" based on his model that spirituality encompasses human potential for life-enhancing experiences of the self, others, God, and nature. In the 2000s, numerous social scientists from Canada and the United States, such as those with backgrounds in social development, human development, and family studies, began to design additional quantitative measures to capture children's spirituality well-being. In addition, social scientists with medical, counseling, or clinical psychology training started to adapt adult measures of RS for use with children and link their self-reported RS to their psychosocial adjustment. Generally, findings have been published in journals that specialize in empirical research on RS, such as the *Psychology of Religion and Spirituality.*

Social scientists and the intergenerational transmission of religion. In contrast to the previous groups, scholars focused on the intergenerational transmission of religion have adhered closely to the language of "religious" or "religion" when examining children's RS. Sociologists have employed national or large regional surveys to document the socialization of worship attendance as well as RS beliefs and practices endorsed by major religious traditions from parents or grandparents to adolescents or young adults. Some leading scholars include Bengtson (Bengtson et al., 2013), Pearce & Denton (2011), Smith & Adamczyk (2021), and numerous other researchers who occasionally publish studies on the intergenerational transmission of RS. Especially relevant to this Element are studies focused on parents' reports of their own role in shaping their children's RS development, with a 2021 book by Smith and Adamczyk epitomizing this work. Mainstream sociology and family journals as well as journals specializing in the science of RS have often been outlets for this work.

Social and cognitive-developmental scientists. A distinctive body of basic research that has steadily gained momentum since the early 2000s involves social and cognitive-developmental scientists examining how children think about supernatural concepts and, especially for this Element, their cognitions about God and prayer. Intersections between attachment theory and RS also fall under the umbrella of social-cognitive developmental research on children's experiences of God. Some leading scholars in this area include Barrett and Richert (Barrett, 2012; Barrett & Richert, 2003; Richert & Smith, 2009), Granqvist (Granqvist, 2020; Richert & Granqvist, 2013), and Lane (Lane, 2020; Lane, Wellman, & Evans, 2010), among numerous others. Initial literature framed findings in terms of children's "religious cognitions," but some work within cognitive and developmental science has shifted toward the language of RS cognitions (Boyatzis, 2013). See Boyatzis (2013), Hood, Hill, and Spilka (2018), and Richert and Granqvist (2013) for chapters that emphasize social and cognitive-developmental research on children's RS. Findings appear in journals focused on child development as well as those specializing in research on RS.

Rising attention to children's RS. As mentioned earlier, scant attention has been paid to children's RS development within the mainstream scientific community that studies children's development. This situation has begun to change, however, with biannual preconferences on children's RS development at the Society for Research in Child Development and several special issues in major journals focused on children's RS development that were championed by Boyatzis (Boyatzis, 2003, 2006; Richert et al., 2017), along with the publication of a handbook on the topic (Roehlkepartain, King, Wagener, & Benson, 2006). The topic has also begun to attract major grant funding, such as funding in 2020 from the Templeton Foundation to build an international community of social scientists to investigate the development of children's RS beliefs across diverse religious contexts and countries, headed by Richert (University of California, 2020).

Children's Wholistic RS Development: Conceptual Models and Measures

Having established the general networks of primarily Western social scientists who conduct empirical research on children's RS development, I turn to a summary of available basic descriptive data about children's reports of their own RS development over time based on global indicators of explicit RS activities or beliefs. Next, I discuss the various conceptual models and measures that quantitative researchers have developed to capture a wholistic description of children's RS functioning. I then highlight areas of convergence and divergence about the nature of "children's spirituality" across these efforts.

Basic Descriptive Information on Children's RS Development

To fully justify using the term "development" when referring to children's RS development in this Element, ample prospective empirical studies would ideally exist that document changes over time in youth (or parent) reports about children's RS experiences from childhood to adolescence or adulthood. Unfortunately, this is not case. I, as well as King and Boyatzis (2015), located only one peer-reviewed published study that tracked changes over time in children's RS (Tamminen, 1994). In this study, youth (ages 7–20) from Finland who belonged to the Lutheran church reported on their experiences of feeling close to God in 1974. The 9- to 10-year-olds ($N = 60$) were reassessed in 1976 and 1980, and they reported significant declines in closeness to God over time. Specifically, 57 percent initially endorsed "yes, very often" about feeling near to God, but these rates dropped to 40 percent by age 11–12 to 18 percent by age 15–16. Cross-sectional comparisons of cohorts by age in 1974 ($N = 1,558$) and in a 1986 replication sample ($N = 1,186$) likewise showed marked shifts downward in felt closeness to God as a function of age. For example, in the 1986 sample, "being alone" was the most common situation where all age groups felt close to God, with 77 percent and 73 percent of the 9- to 10-year-olds and 11- to 12-year-olds "often" or "sometimes" felt near to God during such moments; only 22 percent and 26 percent of the 14- to 15-year olds and 16- to 17-year-olds indicated the same.

Scarce cross-sectional data exist on children's reports of their RS activities based on large, representative samples drawn from anywhere in the world to give perspective on Tamminen's longitudinal findings from data gathered more than forty years ago. A laudable exception is an internet-based survey published in 2010 with a random sample of 1,009 US children between the ages of 8–12 years (Ovwigho & Cole, 2010). The children's three most common religious preferences were Christian Protestant (55 percent), Roman Catholic (15 percent), and atheist or none (11 percent); 31 percent of the children also identified as being "a born-again Christian." For attendance at religious services, 41 percent said they attended weekly, 15 percent once or twice a month, 20 percent less than monthly, and 23 percent never. Although 80 percent reported they prayed daily, only around 30 percent belonged to a religious youth group or read the Bible. Overall, these figures are consistent with US national surveys around 2010 of parents' reports on religious affiliation and worship participation

(Ellison & McFarland, 2013). These similarities are unsurprising because children depend on adults for transportation to RS activities outside the home.

Looking ahead, a key priority for scientific research on children's RS development is collecting basic descriptive information longitudinally and cross-culturally about children's RS. One potential mechanism could be to embed global RS items in quality-of-life measures administered to children. One effort has piloted this strategy with children. Specifically, Jirojanakul and Skevington (2000) included the items "To what extent does your religion make you happy?" and "How satisfied are you with your religious practice (e.g., praying, giving food to a monk, going to a temple, or church, or mosque)?" in a pilot study for assessing quality of life using thirty-five Thai children ages 5–8 years that was modeled after the concepts and procedures based on the World Health Organization's WHOQOL measures (WHOQOL Group, 1995a; 1995b). Otherwise, efforts to include even a few global items on RS when designing cross-cultural studies of children appear to have stalled (https://doi.org/10.1348 /135910700168937)(Cremeens, Eiser, & Blades, 2006; Fisher, 2009). However, global indicators of RS are prevalent in epidemiological and sociological studies of adolescents (Hardy, Nelson, Moore, & King, 2019), and valid subscales on RS have been developed to supplement adults' WHOQOL measures (Hammer, Wade, & Cragun, 2020). Furthermore, Ovwigho and Cole's findings suggest that children can reliably complete global items about RS. Thus, researchers could fruitfully conduct prospective longitudinal surveys to track children's self-reports of developmental changes in their public and private RS activities over time starting around age seven rather than waiting until youth have entered adolescence to establish baseline indicators of RS. Parents could also monitor their children's level of engagement in various RS activities over time.

Wholistic Models and Measures of Children's Spirituality

A handful of efforts have been made to develop wholistic conceptual models of children's RS and create corresponding multidimensional, multi-item self-report measures that are developmentally appropriate for children. A major theme in this literature is a desire to move away from single item indicators of involvement in organized religious groups (e.g., type of affiliation, worship attendance) toward more diverse RS experiences (Fisher, 2009). Table 1 summarizes each research team's abstract conceptual definitions, if provided, of R and S and concrete items used to assess theorized dimensions of children's RS development. To facilitate a later comparative discussion of these models and methods, Table 1 lists the assessment tools on a loose continuum from those that

Table 1. Wholistic Children's RS Models and Measures

Measure and Author	Definition of Religion	Definition of Spirituality	Subscales	Subscale Items
Children's Spiritual Lives (CSS) Moore et al. (2016)	Beliefs, traditions, practices, and ethical codes shared by a particular community	A personal expression of beliefs and values and a relationship with a higher power, regardless of religious affiliation	Comfort	I pray to G-d or talk to G-d when I feel sad. When I want to feel better, I talk or pray to G-d. I ask G-d for help. When I pray to G-d or talk to G-d I feel better about things. G-d helps me by making me feel strong. G-d helps me by making me think of new ideas. I pray to G-d or talk to G-d when I feel sad or worried about something. G-d helps me by giving me advice.

Table 1. (cont.)

Measure and Author	Definition of Religion	Definition of Spirituality	Subscales	Subscale Items
				I pray to G-d because I want to thank G-d for all of the good things in my life.
				When I think about G-d, I feel happy.
				G-d can make people feel better.
				I pray to G-d or talk to G-d when someone is sick or when someone dies.
				G-d keeps people company when they feel sad and lonely.
				G-d listens to my thoughts and wishes.
				I make wishes to G-d and the wishes come true.
			Omnipresence	G-d always knows how I feel, even without talking.

G-d is everywhere in the world and watches over everybody.

G-d created all the people in the world and knows all of them.

I think G-d listens to everyone.

It is impossible for G-d to watch over everybody (reversed item).

There are too many in the world for G-d to know all of them (reversed item).

There are too many people in the world for G-d to listen to (reversed item).

G-d will never know what I am thinking to myself (reversed item).

Dualism

Every person has a body and something inside them, like a soul or spirit.

Table 1. (cont.)

Measure and Author	Definition of Religion	Definition of Spirituality	Subscales	Subscale Items
				People do not have a soul or a spirit (reversed item). Everyone has a body, but having a soul or a spirit is fake (reversed item). I think that people have something like a soul or a spirit that lives inside them.
Youth Spirituality Scale (YSS) Sifers et al. (2012)	Expressing one's faith through prescribed practices, group membership and belief in particular concepts; often includes traditions, rituals, art, and/or symbols	A set of beliefs, practices, or guidelines for behavior and a sense of existential well-being	Relationship with God	How sure are you that there is a God, Higher Power, or Ultimate Reality? How much do you trust God, Higher Power, or Ultimate Reality? How often do you have someone teach you about God, Higher Power, or Ultimate Reality?

How often do you read or listen to books or stories about God, Higher Power, or Ultimate Reality?

*How sure are you that good things will happen in your life?

How sure are you that your God, Higher Power, or Ultimate Reality loves you?

How sure are you that God, Higher Power, or Ultimate Reality is part of your life?

*How sure are you that things happen for a reason?

Religious Practices**

How often do you pray, meditate, or talk to God, Higher Power, or Ultimate Reality?

How often do you want to worship (go to church, temple, synagogue, have ceremonies)?

Table 1. (cont.)

Measure and Author	Definition of Religion	Definition of Spirituality	Subscales	Subscale Items
			Relationship with Others	How often do you follow rules?
				How often are you nice to others?
				How often do you trust that you will be taken care of?
				How often do you treat people like you really care about them?
				How often do you try to do the right thing?
				How often are you thankful?
				How often does someone show you how to be good?
				How often do you apologize?
			Social Desirability Scale	How often do you lie?
				How often do you try to forgive people?

*Items expected to load onto "existential well-being scale" but did not
**Items not anticipated to form a subscale

| Feeling Good, Living | Not defined | A person's awareness of the existence and experience of inner feelings and beliefs, which give purpose, meaning, | Family | (Feeling Good; Living life stems) |
| | | | | Loving/love your family |

Life (FGLL) Fisher (2004)	and value to life; Spirituality helps individuals to live at peace with themselves, to love (God and) their neighbor, and to live in harmony with the environment		Knowing/know your family love you Spending/spend time with your family Knowing/know you belong to a family
		God	Talking/talk with your god Knowing/know your god is a friend Thinking/think about your god Knowing/know your god cares for you
		Nature	Watching/watch a sunset or sunrise Being/be in the garden Going/go for a walk in a park Looking/look at the stars and moon
		Self-Concern	Feeling/feel happy When/hear people say you are good Thinking/think life is fun Knowing/know people like you

Table 1. (cont.)

Measure and Author	Definition of Religion	Definition of Spirituality	Subscales	Subscale Items
Spiritual Sensitivity Scale for Children (SSSC) Stoyles et al. (2012)	Not defined	Spirituality is an innate and unique capacity that is present from an early age, impelling one to move beyond the self in search of meaning and unity through connection with a living world.	Outward Focus	Moments become special because I share them with others, like sharing my birthday with my friends and family. I want to help others. It is important to help people that do not have as much as I do. I think it is important to help others. It is important to make sure my friends and family know that I love them.
			Inward Focus	In a normal day I take time to just think. When I am really concentrating on something, I do not notice other things around me.

I am always learning new things about other people, the world, and myself.

When I am really concentrating on something, I do not notice how much time has passed.

I like to talk about how I am feeling, like if I am feeling happy or sad.

I want to learn more about the world that I live in.

When I am doing something with my hands, I am aware of what my hands are actually feeling.

are the most to least oriented around the assessing God-focused factors, along with other factors the authors theorized to be essential elements of children's spirituality. The later discussion also follows this continuum.

Children's Spiritual Lives. To develop a measure labeled Children's Spiritual Lives (CSL), Moore, Talwar, and Bosacki (2012, p. 219) broadly defined religion "as beliefs, traditions, practices and ethical codes shared by a particular community" and conceptualized spirituality "as a personal expression of beliefs and values and a relationship with a higher power, regardless of religious affiliation." They conducted qualitative semistructured interviews with sixty-four Canadian children (ages 7–11) about spirituality and generated a sixty-four-item survey from coding their responses. They administered this tool to 368 Canadian children who reflected diverse RS backgrounds – 53 percent Christian; 13 percent Jewish; 13 percent Muslim; 6 percent Hindu; 2 percent Other; 11 percent No Religion (Moore, Gomez-Garibello, Bosacki, & Talwar, 2016). Exploratory factor analyses yielded three reliable subscales: (1) a fifteen-item Comfort subscale about turning to God for comfort and help (e.g., seeking help or new ideas, talking or praying, feeling happy or comforted by God); (2) an eight-item Omnipresence subscale about the ubiquity of God (e.g., believing God hears and sees everyone as an all-present creator); and (3) a four-item Duality subscale about having a soul or a spirit apart from the body. Parents also provided two global ratings about the extent to which their family was (1) religious and (2) spiritual. The higher that each of these two parents' ratings were, the higher their children's scores on all three children's CSL factors, with no differences emerging based familial R versus S. For example, children's reports about their views of God or having a soul were comparable for those with parents who identified the family as being "very" religious versus "very" spiritual and "not at all" religious versus "not at all" spiritual. This finding suggests it is premature to pit R against S when studying children's reports of their own RS.

Youth Spirituality Scales. To develop a measure labeled Youth Spirituality Scales (YSS), Sifers, Warren, and Jackson (2012, p. 209) defined faith "as a system of beliefs and values that give meaning to one's life, provide motivation for actions congruent with such beliefs, link individuals with others, and describe the ultimate reality (a deity or eternal truth)." In turn, religion was defined as "expressing one's faith through prescribed practices, group membership, and belief in particular concepts." Spirituality was defined as a "drive to find meaning in one's life and to make sense of one's experiences as they relate to the divine or ultimate reality," which may or may not be a core component of religion. More specifically, the authors stated they generated twenty items based on qualitative descriptions of children's spirituality (Cavalletti, 1992; Coles

1990) and Fowler's (1996, p. 212) definition of spirituality as "a set of beliefs, practices, guidelines for behavior, and a sense of existential well-being."

Sifers et al. administered the YSS to 175 children (ages 7–14) from public schools in a mid-Western area of the United States and conducted an exploratory factor analysis of responses that yielded four subscales: (1) an eight-item Relationship with God subscale concerning learning about "God, Higher Power, or Ultimate Reality" and being certain it is loving and trustworthy, and that good things will happen and events happen for a reason; (2) a two-item Religious Practices subscale about communicating with God, Higher Power, or Ultimate Reality and attending worship services; (3) an eight-item subscale Relationship to Others about prosocial conduct, such as following rules, being nice, and trusting and caring for others; and (4) a two-item social desirability scale. In an online survey of 124 youth (ages 8–15) throughout the United States, the three YSS subscales correlated moderately to highly with the youth reports on RS beliefs, forgiveness, a sense of meaning, organizational religiousness, private religious practices, and RS coping based on items modified from the Brief Multidimensional Measurement of Religiousness-Spirituality (BMMRS), a measure widely used with adults (Idler et al., 2003).

Feeling Good, Living Life. The Feeling Good, Living Life (FGLL; Fisher, 2004) measure is the most extensively researched tool designed to assess children's spirituality. Fisher (1998) built the foundation for FGLL by interviewing ninety-eight secondary teachers from twenty-two nonsectarian and religious schools in Australia about their views of important indicators of spiritual well-being in their students. Their responses led Fisher to develop a wholistic model that conceptualizes "spiritual well-being" as the extent to which people live in harmony within relationships with oneself (personal), others (communal), nature (environment), and God (or transcendental other) (Fisher, Francis, & Johnson, 2000). According to Fisher (1998, 2011), the personal domain involves how individuals view themselves as having a sense of meaning, purpose, and values in life. The communal domain pertains to the quality and depth of relationships to other people, covering love, justice, hope, and faith in humanity. The environmental domain addresses having a sense of connection to nature including a sense of awe, wonder, and unity with the environment. The transcendental other domain involves the individual's felt relationship with something or someone "beyond the human level, such as a cosmic force, transcendent reality, or God," including adoration and worship of such a mysterious force(s). Taken together, Fisher (2011, p. 21) initially defined spirituality as "a person's awareness of the existence and experience of inner feelings and beliefs, which give purpose, meaning and value to life. Spirituality helps individuals to live at peace with themselves, to love (God and) their neighbor, and to live in harmony with the environment." According to Fisher, spirituality could involve an encounter with God, or transcendent reality, in or out of the context of organized religion, but such mystical experiences are not necessary; hence, Fisher placed "God and" in parentheses in his definition of spirituality to account for people who "do not acknowledge a relationship with God." Later, however, Fisher (2015) emphasized that he viewed God as central to children's spiritual well-being.

Fisher first created a questionnaire called the Spiritual Well-Being Questionnaire (SWBQ) to assess adolescents' spiritual well-being according to his four-domain model (Gomez & Fisher, 2003; Moodley, Esterhuyse, & Beukes, 2012) and then designed a parallel tool called Feeling Good, Living Life (FGLL) to be developmentally appropriate for children ages 5 to 12 (Fisher, 2004). Specifically, children report on the extent to which various thoughts and behaviors within the four domains of family, God, nature, and self makes them feel good (i.e., four "feeling good" subscales) and how frequently they engage in the items (i.e., four "live life" subscales). The items are read to children too young to read. Table 1 displays the items for each domain. Two separate domain scores are generated for how good children say they feel when they engage in each activity (e.g., loving your family) and how often they do each activity (e.g., love your family). Consistent with Fisher's model and studies using the SWBQ with adolescents from Australia (Gomez & Fisher, 2003) and South Africa (Moodley et al., 2012), four subscales reliably emerged for each set of "Feel Good" and "Live Life" items based on factor analyses on responses from 1,080 children (ages 5–12) recruited from state, Catholic, independent, and Christian schools in Australia (Fisher, 2004). Subsequent confirmatory factor analyses with responses from three new samples of children from Australia (total $N = 1,455$) reaffirmed that Fisher's four-factor model was a very good fit for the data. Contrary to expectations, however, no consistent differences in domain scores emerged based on children's degree of involvement in religious education.

Spiritual Sensitivity Scale for Children. To develop a measure labeled Spiritual Sensitivity Scale for Children (SSSC), Stoyles, Stanford, Caputi, Keating, and Hyde (2012, p. 204) defined spirituality as "an innate and unique capacity that is present from an early age, impelling one to move beyond the self in search of meaning and unity through connection with a living world." To generate initial items for a quantitative measure to assess children's spiritual sensitivities, the authors turned to Hay and Nye's (1998) and Champagne's (2003) theoretical work on the concept of "relational consciousness," which focuses on children seeking out and recognizing relationships between self and others, and perceiving these relationships as an expression of an outward movement from the child's inner being. The authors further state that children's spirituality sensitivity rests on three fundamental questions: "Who am I?"; "Who am I in relation to other people and the world in which I live?"; and "Who am I in relation to a state of Being that goes beyond the physicality of this world?"

To create the SSSC, the authors conducted a two-phase process with 8- to 11-year-old children who attended three Catholic schools in Australia. They first vetted an initial pool of twenty-three items in focus groups with nineteen children and then administered a twenty-two-item questionnaire to 118 children. As seen in Table 1, the authors ultimately retained twelve items based on a hierarchical cluster analysis that yielded two reliable subscales: (1) a five-item Outward-focused subscale pertaining to helping and having positive relationships with others and (2) a seven-item Inward-focused subscale reflective of being in a flow state and enjoying learning about the world. Higher scores on both subscales correlated, not surprisingly, with children's reports of self-esteem and hope (Stoyles et al., 2012).

Comparing and Critiquing "Children's Spirituality" Models and Measures

A close examination of the four models and tools just discussed offers important insights about areas of convergence and divergence concerning these researchers' views of the nature of "children's spirituality." Similar to adult literature (Nelson, 2009; Oman, 2013), all four models converge in conceptualizing the domain of spirituality as the child's personal expression of internal beliefs and values that presumably give the child a sense of meaning, purpose, and connection to the world outside of the self. Another area of commonality is that all four models give scant attention to children's involvement in organized religious groups or traditions.

The four models on children's spirituality vary as to whether the "something larger than the self" necessarily involves supernatural being(s) or force(s). Researchers use various terms to refer theoretically to supernatural objects of awareness or attachment outside of self, including "God, Higher Power, or Ultimate Reality" (Moore et al., 2012), "the transcendent other" (Fisher, 2004), and "the divine or ultimate reality" (Sifers et al., 2012). The adolescent and adult literature on RS uses these same terms (Exline, 2013; King, Ramos, & Clardy, 2013) plus others, including "the superhuman" in sociology (Smith, 2017) and "the sacred" in psychology (Hill & Pargament, 2008) to refer to self-transcendence as a prototypical feature of spirituality. For individuals following monotheistic (e.g., Christianity, Judaism, Islam) or polytheistic (e.g., Hinduism) religious traditions, the "the sacred" (or "the divine," "the transcendent" or "transcendence," "ultimate reality," "the superhuman," etc.) presumably refers to one or more deities who are in relationship with followers and immanent within humans' lives, although the perceived characteristics of god(s) (and demonic forces) can vary widely across individuals and religious groups. For those affiliated with Buddhism or pantheistic traditions (e.g., Nature oriented, New Age groups), "the sacred" may refer to transpersonal and/or impersonal ultimate realities or truths thought to underlie existence. Pargament and I (2017) have argued that the sphere of "the sacred" can extend beyond the core of "the divine, God, or transcendent reality" and encompass any aspect(s) of life that people perceive as a manifestation of God or embodying sacred qualities often ascribed to the core; these two psychological processes are referred to as theistic and nontheistic sanctification, respectively. A meta-analysis of sixty-three studies of sanctification illustrates that such perceptions are tied to better psychosocial functioning across many domains of life (Mahoney, Wong, Pomerleau, & Pargament, 2021).

Although social scientists use a dizzying array of abstract construct labels to refer to supernatural being(s) or force(s) in conceptual models of spirituality, Table 1 illustrates that the concrete word used quite consistently to operationalize such constructs when measuring "children's spirituality" is "God." Specifically, nearly all of the items on the Comfort and Omnipresence subscales in the CSL, the Relationship with God and Religious Practices subscales in the YSS, and the two God subscales in the FGLL refer to God. Thus, these subscales appear to fall squarely within the domain of RS given that a central mission of most organized religious groups is to facilitate the worship of deities of one type or the other as a source of significance, meaning, purpose, and morality. Furthermore, Fisher (2015) offers a persuasive argument and compelling data that (for children from Western societies steeped in monotheism) the most critical aspects of the FGLL are the two God subscales because children's reports of their frequency and positive feelings about engaging with God explain the greatest amount of variance in the FGLL's overall spiritual well-being score. He also stated that this is the case for adolescents (Fisher, 2015). Nye (2017) has likewise asserted that God is a centerpiece of children's spirituality.

To Fisher's (2015) chagrin and by contrast, the SSSC omits theistic items altogether as a necessary component of spirituality. Some experts on adolescent spiritual development likewise posit that an understanding or experience of "transcendence" per se, including God, a higher power, or other transcendent forces, is not necessary for spiritual development (Roehlkepartain, 2014, p. 6). Rather, Roehlkepartain and colleagues propose that spiritual development is the universal and intrinsic human capacity for self-transcendence, in which the self is embedded in something greater than the self (i.e., "life-writ-large"), as the engine that propels people to seek a sense of connectedness, meaning, purpose, and contribution across the lifespan. This proposition raises challenging conceptual vagueness about the nature of self-transcendence and thus spirituality. What is the nature of the something greater than self that orients the child? Can the "something" be anything outside the self – family, peers, art, sports, music, science, or virtually any cultural phenomenon that fosters a sense of belonging or meaning? Such questions create ambiguity about the boundaries between scientific work on RS and many other social science subfields, such as positive psychology.

A second difficult conceptual issue lurking among the items used in assessment tools based on wholistic models of children's spirituality is that better psychosocial functioning is embedded within many of the subscales. The CSL Comfort scale taps into children reporting feeling better, happier, and stronger by turning to God for help (Moore et al., 2012), and the FGLL Self subscale assesses viewing oneself as well-liked and happy (Fisher, 2004). The YSS Relationship with Others (Sifers et al., 2012) and the SSSY Outward focus subscales tap into children's prosocial behavior toward others, such as being kind, helpful, loving, and well-behaved. The FGLL Family subscale assesses the quality of children's family relationships, including the quality and quantity of time spent together (Fisher, 2004). Thus, authors of these scales all conceptualize children's psychological, social, and moral well-being to be inherent elements of children's RS, three dimensions of psychosocial adjustment that have been studied extensively by developmental, child, and family scientists. However, many social scientists would likely view placing these three facets of children's well-being under the umbrella of spirituality as being an overly inclusive theoretical presumption, even if theologians and religious educators argue that a healthy RS identity necessarily requires virtuous personal and interpersonal functioning. Furthermore, research on adults clearly demonstrates that spiritual struggles with God, demonic forces, morality, and ultimate meaning are tied to worse psychosocial outcomes (Exline, 2013; Exline, Pargament, Grubbs, & Yali, 2014), a possibility that current wholistic models of children's spirituality neglect entirely.

Beyond conceptual conundrums created by theorizing that adaptive psychosocial functioning is an integral component of RS, a third problem arises when researchers claim that RS predicts better psychosocial adjustment of children, but the measures on both sides of the equation are confounded. In other words, employing nearly identical items to assess predictor and outcome variables leads to spurious inferences. For example, a highly cited study used Fisher's

SWBQ with 8- to 12-year-olds and concluded that children's "spirituality well-being" predicted their happiness (Holder, Coleman, & Wallace, 2010). But the specific findings were that child and parental reports of children's happiness were correlated only with children's reports of subjective psychological well-being (i.e., SWBQ personal subscale) and positive interpersonal relationships (i.e., SWBQ communal subscale), net of the effects of school, gender, and temperament. These significant results are consistent with extensive cross-cultural research linking human happiness to higher personal self-esteem and/or quality of social relationships (e.g., Uchida, Norasakkunkit, & Kitayama, 2004). The null results from the felt relationship with God (i.e., SWBQ transcendent subscale) or experiences in nature (i.e., SWBQ environment subscale) subscales could easily raise skepticism as to whether scientific work on children's RS adds unique insights into children's development.

Summary. In this section, I have highlighted challenges that mirror difficulties in conceptualizing what is distinctive about the domain of spirituality for adults (Santos & Michaels, 2020) and the status of adult measures of spirituality (Hill & Edwards, 2013; Kapuscinski & Masters, 2010). Moving forward, social scientists could advance research on children's RS by communicating clearly when desirable child outcomes tied to wholistic RS measures involve children's reports about their felt sense of connection to God (or other perceived supernatural or sanctified objects) versus children's reports on other spiritual well-being subscales that inherently encompass their psychosocial well-being. Such transparency would help integrate findings from this area with the three other bodies of research on children's RS discussed in this Element that focus heavily on concepts of God. Furthermore, with the exception of Stoyles et al. (2012) and Holder et al. (2010), studies still need to be published that document links between the various subscales of wholistic measures of children's spirituality (i.e., CSL, YSS, FGLL, and SSSC) and children's psychosocial functioning.

Children's RS Development: Ties to Psychosocial Adjustment, for Better and Worse

This section of the Element delineates empirical links of children's and parents' RS with children's psychosocial adjustment. Compared to the burgeoning research on adolescents, relatively few studies focus on children as participants. Thus, I first summarize major trends from research on adolescents and offer two major caveats about this literature. These cautions set the stage to examine the studies published in peer-reviewed journals that examine associations of child and parental RS with children's psychosocial adjustment, for better and worse.

Adolescents' RS and Their Psychosocial Adjustment

Major findings regarding desirable outcomes. In the past thirty years, systematic investigation has proliferated on links between adolescents' RS and their psychosocial adjustment up through emerging adulthood (Cheung & Yeung, 2011; Hardy et al., 2019; Pearce, Uecker, & Denton, 2019; Yonker, Schnabelrauch, & DeHaan, 2012). Two meta-analyses exemplify the findings. In seventy-five independent studies published from 1990 to 2010, Yonker et al. (2012) found greater levels of youth RS were modestly correlated with lower risky behavior ($r = -.17$) and depression ($r = -.11$) and greater subjective well-being ($r = .16$) and self-esteem ($r = .11$) as well as higher ratings on three of the "big five" personality traits including conscientiousness ($r = .19$), agreeableness ($r = .18$), and openness ($r = .14$). Focusing on independent effects within forty studies published from 1995 to 2009, Cheung and Yeung (2011) found that greater adolescent RS was correlated with both more constructive functioning ($r = .20$), including volunteer work and concerted study efforts, and avoidance of destructive behavior ($r = .17$), including drug use, theft, drunk driving, risky sexual activity, and delinquency. Both of these meta-analyses as well as Hardy et al.'s (2019) narrative review of 241 studies published from 1988 to 2107 concluded that private indicators of RS activity, such as prayer or turning to God for support, were more robustly tied to outcomes than public RS measures, such as religious affiliation or worship attendance. Furthermore, Hardy et al. (2019) noted that twelve longitudinal studies suggest that RS may causally protect youth from negative outcomes (e.g., risk behaviors and mental illness) and promote prosocial development.

In a theoretical synthesis of this literature, Pearce et al. (2019) suggested that greater RS helps to shape adolescents' moral schemas that, in turn, influence their related attitudes and behaviors. Evidence includes that higher RS has been tied to inhibited sexual activity outside of marriage, lower alcohol and substance use, greater self-regulation, more control of impulses and emotions, and higher self-efficacy, self-concept, locus of control, a strong sense of self or meaning, and compassion for others. In addition, higher adolescent RS has been tied to learned competencies to cope effectively with stressors and engage in constructive leadership roles, such as being more active in school or civic volunteer organizations. Finally, higher RS covaries with adolescents' access to social networks including positive peer, parental, and other adult role models. Such social capital can provide teens with emotional support, guidance in achieving educational and professional goals, and facilitate mature decision making.

Caveat 1: Are the muddled middle most at risk? Overall, social scientists appear willing to venture a "yes, weakly" to the question "Are higher levels of RS correlated with psychosocial benefits for adolescents?" However, in addition to the conspicuous need for more longitudinal and experimental studies, one key caveat about this conclusion comes from sophisticated person-centered profile analyses of teens and young adults in the United States. This work suggests that psychosocial adjustment is actually poorest for those who consistently fall in the moderate range on various dimensions of RS compared to individuals who uniformly adhere to high or low RS beliefs and practices (Barry, Christofferson, Boorman, & Nelson, 2020; Longo, Bray, & Kim-Spoon, 2017; Nadal, Hardy, & Barry, 2018). For example, in a national sample of US university students (ages 18–25; $N = 9,495$), those with *either* a high or low RS profile reported higher identity maturity and psychological well-being and lower depression, alcohol use, and risky sexual activity compared to the moderate RS group (Nadal et al., 2018). Similarly, Appalachian adolescents ($N = 220$; ages 12–18) whose person-centered latent profiles consistently reflected *either* high or low patterns of RS had lower internalizing and externalizing symptomatology compared to the middle-range group (Longo et al., 2017). Using data from the National Study of Youth and Religion (NSYR) project, Pearce and Denton (2011) generated five distinct profiles based on surveys completed in 2002–03 by a representative sample of US 13- to 17-year-olds ($N = 3,290$). They found that Abiders (22 percent) who consistently and highly endorsed conventional markers of RS as well as Atheists (3 percent) who clearly did the opposite were less depressed and had higher educational goals by 2005 compared to the bulk of teens whose RS profiles were marked by less coherence, such as less conventionality (Adapters, 28 percent), centrality (Assenters, 30 percent), and/or clarity and comfort in how RS fits into their lives (Avoiders, 17 percent).

At least three reasons may account for why a more ambivalent stance toward RS could place adolescents at the highest risk of psychosocial difficulties compared to teens who firmly either reject RS or embrace RS at high doses (Barry et al., 2020; Nadal et al., 2018). First, those in the middle may experience more problematic RS struggles and doubts that are reciprocally tied to negative psychosocial functioning (Exline, 2013; Exline, Yali, & Sanderson, 2000). Second, compared to their non-RS peers, teens in the middle range may experience more cognitive dissonance that generates psychospiritual distress when they engage in culturally normative behavior that violates traditional RS moral rules (e.g., prohibited sexual activity or alcohol use). Third, compared to high RS peers who are more likely to adhere faithfully and happily to RS precepts, adolescents in the middle may experience more moments of distressing moral incongruence because their behavior more often violates their own or their family's professed RS beliefs. Overall, youth may be best served by helping them develop either a coherent and well-integrated RS or non-RS identity that sidesteps problematic RS struggles.

Caveat 2: Disentangling positive and negative manifestations of RS. Another caution that major reviews on research of RS and adolescent health highlight is that malignant manifestations of RS, although relatively rare, tend to intensify psychosocial problems. Yet, most studies use global items to assess RS that obscure what can help or harm. Examples of global indicators include frequency of religious affiliation, attendance, and overall importance of religion or spirituality. Cotton, McGrady, and Rosenthal (2006) found that two-thirds of studies of youth RS and their physical or mental health used only one or two such items. Most multi-item measures also simply add more questions about public or private RS activities without specifying the substantive content of participants' RS thoughts or feelings that could be adaptive or maladaptive (Cheung & Yeung, 2011). Such vagueness leaves much room for skeptics to take a selectively reductionist stance about salutary implications of RS. Specifically, skeptics can argue that any apparent benefits of greater RS activity merely reflect basic psychosocial mechanisms, such as meaning-making or social support, rather than tapping into anything conceptually unique about RS, such as feeling a profound sense of comfort from a loving deity or perceptions of the sanctity of an aspect of life. On the other hand, skeptics can easily attribute significant correlations of global RS indices with undesirable consequences to substantive RS factors, such as belief that a deity or passages of scripture condone problematic conduct, even if those problematic RS processes are not directly assessed (Cotton et al., 2006; Mahoney, 2013). In addition, global RS items can allow researchers with an indiscriminately proreligious theoretical lens to accentuate only the benefits of RS because global indices tend to conceal rare but toxic forms of faith, especially in large national or community samples of nondistressed individuals.

Solutions to two caveats. Social scientists who would like to offer practitioners and policy makers balanced insights for prevention and intervention programs aimed at youth need studies that disentangle RS resources that ameliorate psychosocial distress from RS struggles that can amplify psychopathology (Hardy et al., 2019; Mahoney, Pomerleau, & Riley, 2019; Pearce et al., 2019). For example, in a longitudinal study with 760 US adolescents (ages 16–18) belief in a loving God predicted less aggressive and more benevolent behavior (helping and forgiveness) six and twelve months later, whereas belief in a punitive God (10 percent of sample) corresponded with more aggressive and less benevolent behavior over time (Shepperd, Pogge, Lipsey, Miller, &

Webster, 2019). Similar opposing processes can occur with youth's connections to religious congregations. For instance, among 12- to 15-year-olds (N = 744, US New England area), anticipating positive support from their religious congregations in times of need was uniquely tied to lower depressive symptoms; conversely, expectations of being criticized were tied to increased depressive symptoms after taking into account overall RS and public and private RS practices (Pearce, Little, & Perez 2003). With these two caveats in mind based on adolescent research, this Element now delves into peer-reviewed quantitative studies using children's reports of RS.

Children's RS and Their Psychosocial Adjustment

Global RS and children in nondistressed community samples. A handful of studies have linked children's own responses on global RS items to their psychosocial adjustment based on nondistressed community samples. Using the largest and most representative US sample in this literature, Ovwigho and Cole (2010) found that 8- to 12-year-old US children's self-reports of attending any place of worship was tied to lower risky health behaviors, including smoking, drinking alcohol, engaging in sexual activity, viewing pornography, and "sexting." Specifically, 11.3 percent of those who attended services at least once a month versus 24.3 percent of lower attenders engaged in at least one of these problematic behaviors. Moreover, this association held after controlling for age, gender, and the study's three other global RS factors (i.e., prayer, Bible reading, and identifying as a born-again Christian), none of which uniquely predicted these risky behaviors. For commonplace acts of relational aggression (e.g., gossiping, lying), the sole unique RS predictor was reading the Bible at least four times a week. Notably, only 9 percent of the children read the Bible this often. This finding highlights the importance of a high "dosing effect." Specifically, 56 percent of this small group of devout children engaged in relational aggression compared to 64 percent and 68 percent of the bulk of children who either never or read the Bible up to three times per week.

Focusing on children (ages 6–12, N = 328) from predominantly evangelical Christian backgrounds, Crosby and Smith (2017) assessed children's perceptions of their self-disclosure with people in the church community as well as social support from peers and adults from their church. After conducting initial psychometric analyses with the entire sample, the authors examined a subsample of fifty children enrolled in one Christian school. They found that three church-engagement subscales each uniquely predicted children's self-esteem and prosocial behavior after controlling for global RS (religious affiliation, attendance, and education) and other sources of social support from home and school. In another study using structural equation modeling (SEM), Smith and Crosby (2017) found that Christian children (ages 7–12, N = 844) from southern and midwestern regions of the United States who reported more social support from peers from their church and a positive relationship with God also reported greater self-esteem. Children's positive relationship with God also mediated the indirect pathways in the SEM model from their family's religious practices and social support from adults from their church to their self-esteem.

Inconsistent findings have emerged using global RS indicators to predict children's happiness. Children (ages 8–12; N = 320) attending public and private religious schools in Australia completed eleven items from the adult BMMRS encompassing worship attendance, prayer, reading religious material, feeling close to a loving and protective higher power, and using RS to cope with problems (Holder et al., 2010). These items were summed and found to be unrelated to parental and child reports of the child's happiness. For children from Zambia (ages 7–12, N = 391), their reports of religious attendance and overall salience of RS were tied to some, but not other, indicators of their happiness (Holder, Coleman, Krupa, & Krupa, 2016).

One intriguing study honed in on children's reports of their positive attitudes about belonging to an organized religious community while living in the Netherlands, a highly secularized country. Oulali et al. (2019) designed a measure that asks children if they identify with a religious group by filling in the blank in this statement: I consider myself to be _____ (e.g., Christian, Hindu, Muslim, Jewish). Children then responded to other questions about their private religious collective self-esteem in being part of their group (i.e., does child feel good, proud, annoyed about being ____), public religious collective esteem based on other children's reactions about that group (e.g., do other children feel good, find it strange or annoying, and respect the child belonging to that group), and importance of religious identity (e.g., does the child feel belonging to the group is important and matters). Students (ages 11–12; N = 680) were recruited from public and private school. Forty-seven percent identified as Muslim, 31 percent as Christian, 19 percent as Hindu, and 3 percent as another religion. As expected, more positive and intense identification with their religious group was moderately associated with higher personal and ethnic self-esteem. This tool offers an innovative way to conduct cross-cultural research on ways children may reconcile conflicting thoughts and feelings about their RS identity, especially those immigrating into environments that are more secular.

Finally, a unique study of children attending Catholic or Protestant schools (age 11; N = 2,586) in West Scotland further highlights RS cultural context issues (Abbotts, Williams, Sweeting, & West, 2004). For all children, weekly church attendance was tied to less self-reported fighting and aggressive behavior reported by teachers and parents. However, internalizing problems showed a different pattern. Weekly attendance that was normative for Catholic children was tied to better self-esteem and less anxiety and depression. By contrast, weekly attendance by affiliates of the Church of Scotland was much less typical and tied to poorer self-esteem, more anxiety, and depression with evidence that the Protestant children were subjected to more teasing by their Protestant peers due their nonnormative RS behavior.

Global RS and children living in stressful situations. A few studies have addressed whether higher overall RS helps children cope with stressful life events. Some have yielded encouraging findings, as follows. Davis and Epkins (2009) examined whether, among preadolescents from Lubbock, Texas (ages 11–12; $N = 160$), the frequency of worship services and private religious practices (i.e., prayer or meditation, reading or listening to religious media) moderated the correlation between maternal and self-reported family conflict and internalizing symptoms. Neither type of RS activity was directly tied to depressive and anxiety symptoms. However, greater family conflict was far more predictive of internalizing symptoms for children who rarely engaged in private religious practices compared to weak or null associations for children who often used RS resources. Rew, Wong, and Sternglanz (2004) selected the 271 children (ages 9–12) living in Texas from the larger sample ($N = 1,024$) who either said that they both prayed "most of the time" and that "it helps a lot" versus those who "never" prayed as a coping mechanism. The former group reported a greater use of humor to cope, social support from adults, and healthy lifestyle behaviors (e.g., teeth-brushing, healthy diet, seat belts). Howell, Shapiro, Layne, and Kaplow (2015) examined the adaptive functioning of fifty-six parentally bereaved children (ages 7–13) who had lost their caregiver in the previous six months. Adaptive functioning was defined as falling below clinical threshold levels of psychopathology as reported by children and caregivers (57 percent of sample). Among numerous salient resources, children in the adaptive functioning group reported higher religious attendance and higher scores on a seventeen-item omnibus RS measure presumed to reflect RS coping.

Other studies offer little evidence that higher global RS buffers distressed children from maladjustment. Kim, McCullough, and Chicchetti (2009) obtained two complex and counterintuitive interactive effects between parents' and children's (ages 6–12) reports on two global RS items and children's psychological adjustment for 159 maltreated versus 170 nonmaltreated children. Namely, only among the nonmaltreated children who rarely attended worship services, parents' frequent attendance and importance of faith was related to children's lower internalizing symptomatology, and parents' importance of faith was associated with lower externalizing symptomatology.

Otherwise, null results emerged, yielding a very difficult pattern of findings to interpret clearly. Also, among clinic-referred children (ages 10–12; $N = 543$) from the Netherlands diagnosed with mental health problems, only one significant association emerged among child, maternal, and paternal reports of their global RS and all three parties as well as teacher reports of child externalizing and internalizing symptoms (Van der Jagt-Jelsma et al., 2015); greater maternal RS was tied to mothers' higher reports of child internalizing symptoms. A follow-up longitudinal study yielded null findings for RS variables (Van der Jagt-Jelsma et al., 2017).

Overall, inconclusive findings link global RS factors to better psychosocial adjustment for children, especially those facing serious life stressors. Moving forward, studies are needed to explicitly assess helpful and harmful functions of RS for children living in adverse circumstances.

Positive and negative RS coping. Rooted in Pargament's (1997) seminal book on RS coping, extensive research exists on this topic for adults (Abu-Raiya & Pargament, 2015) that needs to be extended to youth (Mahoney, Pendleton, & Ihrke, 2006). Measures of positive RS coping largely tap into the extent to which people draw on a benevolent and secure relationship with God (i.e., divine coping), along with a sense of spiritual support from co-believers, to cope with stressful events. Such processes have been tied to better adult health and psychological adjustment (Abu-Raiya & Pargament, 2015; Pargament, 1997). Negative RS coping refers to ways that stressors trigger distressing RS thoughts and feelings about supernatural figures (e.g., anger toward God, feeling punished by the Devil), religious groups (e.g., conflicts with co-believers), or the self (e.g., feeling morally conflicted or confused about ultimate meaning). These processes have been increasingly referred to as "spiritual struggles" since Exline et al. (2014) created six subscales that differentiate divine (i.e., God-focused), demonic struggles, and RS-based conflicts with other people from moral, intrapsychic, and existential struggles that do not necessarily involve supernatural figures. Cross-sectional and longitudinal studies with adults suggest that RS struggles generally lead to declines in physical, psychological, and RS well-being, particularly if left unresolved, but occasionally promote personal growth if they are resolved (Abu-Raiya & Pargament, 2015; Exline, 2013; Exline et al., 2014).

Compelling qualitative accounts from medically ill children (e.g., Pendleton, Cavalli, Pargament, & Nasr, 2002) and adults' retrospective narratives of traumatic childhood experiences (e.g., Bryant-Davis, Ellis, Burke-Maynard, Moon, Counts, & Anderson 2012) indicate that children can experience both positive and negative RS coping processes. The two published studies on RS coping that have included children illustrate the urgent need for more science on this topic. First, in an exemplary longitudinal study of eighty-seven youth (ages 8–17) hospitalized for severe asthma (Benore, Pargament, & Pendleton, 2008), negative RS coping robustly predicted poorer adjustment during hospitalization and at a one-month follow-up after controlling for secular coping strategies and other relevant controls. Contrary to expectations, positive RS coping also predicted increased anxiety cross-sectionally and longitudinally. Second, Van Dyke, Glenwick, Cecero, and Kim (2009) surveyed seventy-six preadolescent and early adolescent youth (ages 11–14) living in an inner-city, low-income environment in the United States. Greater positive RS coping was weakly tied to more life satisfaction and positive affect but unrelated to psychological distress. By contrast, greater negative RS coping was robustly linked to greater depression, anxiety, and somatization symptoms and significantly predicted psychological distress after controlling for gender, grade, positive RS coping, and global RS experiences.

Summary of children's RS and psychological adjustment. Together, initial findings paint a less clear-cut picture that children's reports of global RS are tied to their well-being compared to burgeoning evidence of salutary, albeit modest, associations for adolescents. Although some parallel positive associations have emerged based on children's reports of global RS, many null or conflicting findings exist. Furthermore, initial evidence suggests that children living in stressful situations may often find that increased efforts to turn to RS to cope do not reduce their psychological distress that could be further aggravated by distressing RS struggles. More research is imperative to help adults help children grapple with both the bright and dark sides of RS when trouble strikes children's lives.

Parents' RS, Parenting, and Children's Psychosocial Adjustment

An extensive body of research speaks to ways RS may influence becoming and being a parent across infancy, childhood, and adolescence. It is well beyond the scope of this Element to delineate these myriad findings (see Mahoney & Boyatzis, 2019; Mahoney, 2010; Marks & Dollahite, 2016). In brief, based predominantly on cross-sectional data from US samples, greater parental RS has been consistently tied to women's stronger motivations to bear children as well as to married heterosexuals and single mothers' greater satisfaction and self-efficacy about being a parent, parental warmth and investment, positive parenting strategies, and parents' commitment to their preferred discipline strategies when rearing school-age children. Although these findings imply that parental RS would directly and indirectly lead to children's better psychosocial adjustment via better parenting (Hardy,

Dollahite & Baldwin, 2019; Mahoney & Boyatzis, 2019), studies that directly examine such pathways defy easy generalizations. Instead, surprisingly complex linkages exist among parental RS, parenting practices, and children's adjustment. To provide a sufficient and broad context for understanding the complicated linkages between parental RS and children's adjustment, I first summarize the scarce longitudinal work on parental RS tied to adolescent outcomes via parenting.

Longitudinal Research on Parental RS with Adolescents

Three exemplary longitudinal studies show that higher parental RS in households with adolescents predicts better personal psychosocial functioning of teens directly and via parenting. Spilman, Neppl, Donnellan, Schofield, and Conger (2013) conducted a twenty-year study across three generations of two-parent families ($N = 451$) from rural Iowa using direct observations of marital and parent-offspring interactions. Couples with higher self-reported RS initially demonstrated more positive parenting (and marital) functioning during their adolescent's high school years, which, in turn, was tied to their offspring later exhibiting more positive parenting with their grandchildren. In a national survey of two-parent US households (Li, 2013), parents' RS was directly tied to 12- to 14-year-olds ($N = 2,922$) engaging in less delinquent behavior two years later. Moreover, parental RS indirectly predicted less delinquency by increasing teens' perceptions of less interparental conflict, better parenting practices, and stronger affection for parents; preliminary analyses found similar results with single-parent households. In another longitudinal study of 612 African American families (Landor, Simons, Simons, Brody, & Gibbons, 2011), greater parental RS predicted 15- to 16-year-olds engaging in less risky sexual behavior (early sexual debut, multiple sexual partners, and inconsistent condom use) two years later. Parental RS indirectly influenced teen behavior by increasing authoritative parenting, adolescent religiosity, and teens' avoidance of sexually permissive peers. Overall, these longitudinal studies suggest that parental RS can enhance adolescents' future adjustment via better parenting. Mediational modeling also helps offset (though does not completely eliminate) concerns that selection effects or third variables fully account for cross-sectional evidence tying greater parental RS to desirable parenting practices with this age group. However, four longitudinal studies with families with children yield a far more complicated picture about how parental RS influences children's adjustment, for better and worse.

Parental RS and Children's Adjustment

Longitudinal research on global parental RS and children's adjustment.
Bornstein et al. (2017) conducted a three-year longitudinal investigation of
1,198 families from nine countries, spanning four religions (Catholicism,
Protestantism, Buddhism, and Islam) plus unaffiliated parents; nearly all families included a mother and father (91 percent), with nearly a third having three
or more adults (31 percent). The researchers assessed parental self-reports of the
overall importance of religion in their lives and how much their religious beliefs
influenced their parenting. On a positive note, greater parental RS at a child age
eight predicted higher parental efficacy and warmth at child age nine; both of
these parenting factors, in turn, increased children's social competence and
school performance at age ten. On a less desirable note, greater parental RS at
child age eight predicted stronger parent behavioral control of youth with little
opportunity for autonomy at child age nine, which in turn was associated with
more child internalizing and externalizing problems at age ten, although the
children's difficulties fell below clinical levels of distress. Greater parental RS
was also tied to children's – but not parents' – reports of parental rejection,
which in turn was associated with increases in children's adjustment difficulties
at age ten. Importantly, none of these effects were moderated by parents'
gender, religious group affiliation, or nationality, and child gender.

After obtaining positive cross-sectional associations between parents' RS
and better child behavioral, emotional, and cognitive development in a national
US sample of families headed by married heterosexuals (Bartkowski, Xu, &
Levin, 2008), a longitudinal study ($N = 10,700$) using the same data set yielded
a complex mix of mostly null or adverse effects, with few desirable outcomes.
Specifically, Bartkowski, Xu, and Bartkowski (2019) examined parents' reports
of their worship attendance as well as the parent-child discussions and parental
arguments about RS at home when their children were 6- to 7-years-old and
gathered parent and teacher reports of children's psychosocial and academic
functioning at child age 6–7 (time 1) and again at 8–9 (time 2). Contrary to
expectations, lower parental conflict about RS did not longitudinally predict any
child outcomes, and none of the RS variables predicted child externalizing
behavior problems, net of baseline functioning. Unexpectedly, more frequent
parent-child discussion about RS longitudinally predicted children's lower
reading achievement scores and otherwise were only tied to their better interpersonal skills. The authors also extensively examined each parent's frequency
of worship attendance as well as the couples' attendance as a unit (frequently,
semi-regularly, sporadically) compared to couples who never attended.
Contrary to expectations, couples who semi-attended services together had

children with the best outcomes. This RS variable led over time to more child self-control and interpersonal skills, less internalizing problems, and better learning skills (e.g., persistence, effort, organization) compared to nonattending couples, with no advantages for children whose parents frequently attended services together. Furthermore, children's later scientific test scores were lower for all families where couples who attended services were compared to non-attending families. For individual parental attendance, no consistent effects emerged. Specifically, higher maternal attendance predicted lower reading proficiency and math acumen, and higher paternal attendance predicted lower internalizing problems and better learning skills, but no other child outcomes.

Substantive RS messages about parenting and opposing child outcomes. Overall, global markers of familial RS in two-parent households predict complex and often undesirable child outcomes based on available longitudinal studies. These mixed results may be due to the wide range of substantive RS messages that parents may internalize about child-rearing goals and strategies when exposed to varying RS teachings (Holden & Vittrup, 2010; Mahoney & Boyatzis, 2019; Starks & Robinson, 2007). Diverse religious groups encompass progressive to conservative theological positions on social, political, and existential issues; wide variation exists both within and between religious denominations on controversial moral and ethical issues pertinent to parenting (Onedera, 2008; Starks & Robinson, 2007). Parents can selectively seek support from religious subgroup(s) that informs and reinforces their preferred parenting methods and desired child outcomes (Mahoney & Boyatzis, 2019). For instance, in Bartkowski et al. (2019), the married co-parents who very frequently attended services at either end of the progressive-conservative continuum may have canceled out their potentially opposing effects of permissive versus rigid parenting, leaving behind U-shaped findings due to the semiregular attenders. However, consistent with the strong pro-science education stance typically taken by parents who never attend religious services, the children of these parents had uniformly higher scientific achievement scores compared to children of parents who attended services at any level (Bartkowski et al., 2019).

Clearly, as is the case with children's RS, more research is needed on substantive RS messages about parenting that parents may absorb from various sources. Along these lines, the potential role that conservative RS beliefs play in promoting corporal punishment has been the one topic of persistent attention by social scientists for several decades (Holden & Williamson, 2014; Mahoney, Pargament, Swank, & Tarakeshwar, 2001; Mahoney, 2010).

Conservative RS, corporal punishment, and child adjustment. Parents in the United States who self-identify as conservative Protestants (e.g., Southern

Baptist, evangelical, or nondenominational Christian) and/or interpret the Bible literally are more likely to advocate and use corporal punishment with their children compared to nonaffiliates and parents from other Christian or non-Christian groups (Ellison, Bartkowski, & Segal, 1996; Ellison & Bradshaw, 2009; Ellison, Musick, & Holden, 2011). Furthermore, cross-sectional data from US General Social Surveys (GSS) from 1986 to 2014 reveals that support for corporal punishment has remained robust among less educated Conservative Protestant Christians (CPC), with growing erosion among more highly educated CPCs (Hoffmann, Ellison, & Bartkowski, 2017). CPC beliefs or affiliations also predict parents' use of corporal punishment in the United States (Ellison et al., 2011, Mahoney et al., 2001, 2010; Petts, 2012) and Canada (Frechette & Romano, 2015). In addition, more religiously conservative Jewish mothers and fathers in Israel are more likely than others to use corporal punishment, with devout fathers who have a genetic predisposition toward aggression and aggressive children especially likely to use corporal punishment (Avinun, Davidov, Mankuta, & Knafo-Noam, 2018).

These findings have sparked heated debates about the adverse impact, or not, of corporal punishment on children's well-being over time within RS conservative families who value this disciplinary strategy (Dyslin & Thomsen, 2005; Holden & Williamson, 2014). A careful look at three published studies on the effects of physical discipline on children within RS families is instructive. First, using longitudinal data gathered between 1987 and 1994, Ellison et al. (2011) found that US 2- to 4-year-olds of CPC mothers exhibited minimal negative effects of corporal punishment five years later and less antisocial behavior if CPC mothers discontinued spanking as their children matured. Second, updating this study with longitudinal data collected between 2001 and 2005 on two-parent families, Petts and Kysar-Moon (2012) found US preschoolers to be less likely to display misbehavior over time in a very specific family context if only the father spanked and spanked infrequently, and both parents were conservative Protestants. In the bulk of two-parent families who did not conform to these narrow parameters, spanking predicted greater negative child outcomes, as has been documented more generally (Gershoff, Goodman, Miller-Perrin, Holden, Jackson, & Kazdin, 2018). Notably, Mahoney and Boyatzis (2019) pointed out that only about 11 percent of US families with minor youth (age up to 18) are headed by married heterosexuals who are both evangelical Protestants. In short, a small minority of US households with young children fits the family context where corporal punishment may co-occur in a broader set of CPC beliefs that may offset the typically adverse effects of physical discipline.

A third cross-sectional study on parental RS tied to child problems via corporal punishment underscores the need for more broadscale research.

Specifically, Alsarhi, Rahma, Prevoo, Alink, and Mesman (2019) gathered innovative data on Muslim mothers living with 2- to 6-year-olds in slums in Yemen. Mothers' greater use of harsh physical discipline during an observed child compliance task was robustly tied to maternal reports of more child behavior problems, but only for mothers who frequently drew on RS beliefs to explain their reactions to vignettes depicting children transgressing Islamic rules. One intriguing speculation for these findings was that children might suffer more emotional distress and anger in family contexts where parents more often evoke God, prayer, or other RS concepts (e.g., heaven, hell) to shame children and justify harsh parenting. It is unknown how pervasive such practices are currently, but several decades ago 27 percent of school-aged children from mid-Western United States reported that at least one of their parents told them God would punish them if they were bad (Nelsen & Kroliczak, 1984).

Parental RS attendance and corporal punishment. Given the concern of developmental scientists that conservative RS fosters harsh parenting practices, it may be surprising to learn that greater religious participation by parents at any place of worship has repeatedly been tied to *less*, not more, use of corporal punishment (Mahoney, 2010; Mahoney & Boyatzis, 2019). For example, in a longitudinal study of single US mothers, multiple trajectories of higher maternal religious attendance (i.e., consistent frequent, moderate, or monthly attenders and high-increasing attenders) predicted lower corporal punishment over time compared to nonattending mothers (Petts, 2012). Higher worship attendance was also tied to lower corporal punishment in separate cross-sectional analyses of Canadian parents (mostly married and female) of children ages 2–5 years, 6–9 years, and 10–11 years (Frechette & Romano, 2015) over the years from 1994 to 2009 (*NS* varied between 5,531 and 12,431). Similarly, a twelve-item measure of positive RS experiences (e.g., I feel God's love for me, directly; I find strength in my RS) correlated with lower rates of spanking and slapping children by 294 Ukrainian mothers (71 percent married/partnered) (Grogan-Kaylora, Burlakab, Mac, Leea, Castilload, & Churakovab, 2018). However, Silveira, Shafer, Dufur, and Roberson (2020) examined national data sets of children (ages 7–9) from the United Kingdom (*N* = 11,113) and United States (*N* = 13,008) and found that greater parental religious attendance correlated with more spanking or hitting as a discipline strategy, net of parent ethnicity, age, education, income, and depression; family structure and size; and child age, gender, behavioral, and emotional problems. Similar to prior findings from the United States (Mahoney & Boyatzis, 2019), greater religious attendance was also tied to US parents more often using positive discipline strategies, such as withdrawal of privileges and reasoning and discussing misbehavior, but not UK parents.

Parental RS and child maltreatment. Social scientists have often raised the concern that conservative RS beliefs about parenting heighten the risk of child maltreatment (Holden & Vittrup, 2010; Holden & Williamson, 2014). Contrary to this hypothesis, a study of 313 counties drawn from seven geographically diverse US states documented that rates of child physical abuse were lower, not higher, in counties that had higher levels of Christian conservativism (Breyer & MacPhee, 2015). Two in-depth studies have further pinpointed the use of RS for instrumental purposes (i.e., extrinsic religiousness) as a key predictor of greater risk of child physical abuse, not type of religious affiliation, orthodox religious beliefs, or the centrality of religion to one's identity (i.e., intrinsic religiousness) (Dyslin & Thomsen, 2005; Rodriguez & Hendersen, 2010). Additionally, in studies of low-income or ethnic minority US mothers, higher importance of RS has been repeatedly tied to a lower risk of child maltreatment or harsh parenting (Mahoney, 2010; Mahoney et al., 2001). Higher religious attendance also emerged as a protective factor against child physical abuse in three early rigorous longitudinal studies (Mahoney et al., 2001).

Summary of parental RS and children's adjustment. This portion of the Element has summarized complex evidence suggesting that parental RS can shape children's adjustment for better and worse. More research is needed across varying family and cultural contexts to identify substantive RS beliefs parents may embrace that directly or indirectly influence children's adjustment by intensifying helpful and harmful parenting practices. More studies are especially needed that untangle specific RS beliefs that encourage and discourage corporal punishment and child maltreatment across diverse faith communities around the globe.

Parental RS Coping with Challenging Children

Some scientific attention has addressed whether positive RS coping could help parents living with more challenging children. Unexpectedly, however, in cross-sectional studies with parents with at-risk preschoolers ($N = 149$; Dumas & Nissley-Tsiopinis, 2006) and children with autism ($N = 45$; Tarakeshwar & Pargament, 2001), parents' positive RS coping methods were unrelated to parental attitudes or behaviors. Such null findings may reflect stress-mobilization coping processes where parents more often seek strength from God when they feel taxed or overwhelmed. Consistent with this notion, Schottenbauer, Spernak, and Hellstrom (2007) examined the parents' use of prayer/meditation and putting trust in a higher power to cope using US national data from families with 8- to 9-year-olds formerly enrolled in early education programs for disadvantaged youth ($N = 7$, $N = 7,515$). Together these RS coping strategies correlated with greater parental nurturance, consistency, and nonrestrictive attitudes and predicted children's better social skills, after controlling for positive parenting. However, often putting trust in a higher power also uniquely predicted greater child hyperactivity and externalizing behavior problems, consistent with a stress-mobilization dynamic. In addition, positive RS coping by parents from the mid-Western United States ($N = 136$) was related to higher self-appraisals of competence when parents perceived their children as having more behavior problems (Weyand, O'Laughlin, & Bennett, 2013). Overall, parents with more difficult children may more often draw on RS coping to bolster their resilience and confidence in their preferred parenting methods, with uneven results.

On the flip side, greater RS struggles have been linked to parental depression and distress for parents of at-risk preschoolers (Dumas & Nissley-Tsiopinis, 2006) and children with autism (Tarakeshwar & Pargament, 2001). Also, greater parental RS has been correlated with greater depressive symptoms in parents caring for children with developmental disabilities and, in follow-up qualitative interviews, these parents reported struggling to turn to God as a last resort to cope with feeling overwhelmed (Gallagher, Phillips, Lee, et al., 2015). In addition, children diagnosed with chronic disabilities are less likely to attend religious services, suggesting that they and their families may more often face stigma or rejection in religious contexts than other types of families (Whitehead, 2018).

Summary of parental RS coping. Overall, as is the case for children's RS coping (Mahoney et al., 2006), more studies are merited on distressed families where parents may be more alienated from valuable RS resources and vulnerable to painful RS struggles because both processes could heighten parental despair and undermine parenting (for fuller discussion, see Mahoney & Boyatzis, 2019). Such research could pinpoint aspects of RS that differentially lead to desirable and undesirable psychosocial outcomes for children and their families.

Intergenerational Transmission of RS to Children

This Element now shifts to family factors thought to contribute to children's RS development. Specifically, this section addresses scientific research on the intergenerational transmission from parents to children of RS (non)affiliation with major world religions and associated beliefs and practices. I first summarize numerous quantitative studies showing that parents are highly influential in whether their adolescents or young adults adopt or reject their RS affiliation, attitudes, or practices. Then, I summarize qualitative reports of RS-engaged parents from diverse family structures who voice similar goals and strategies so their young children have access to RS resources to help them become happy and good people. I close by introducing work that indicates that children can countershape their parents' RS lives.

Quantitative Evidence on the Intergenerational Transmission of RS

Overall intergenerational transmission of RS. A recent meta-analysis provides concise and informative insights on the empirical connection between parental and youth RS (Stearns & McKinney, 2019a). The authors located thirty studies published between 1990 and 2017 with correlational data using parent, adolescent, or emerging adult reports of global RS. Most studies relied on US samples composed predominantly of participants affiliated with a Christian tradition, and many used data collected at least fifteen years ago. These are important details given rapidly shifting trends in the United States where contemporary adults report being markedly less RS than prior generations during early adulthood (Exline et al., 2014). Overall, a robust effect size of $r = .49$ emerged between parent-offspring RS in the meta-analysis. This finding converges with social scientists' long-standing consensus that parents are the most powerful and proximal influence on adolescent RS (Bengtson et al., 2013; Smith & Adamczyk, 2021). Replication studies using children's reports of RS are needed, especially given surprisingly weak or null linkages between parental RS and children's attachment to God (Cassiba, Granqvist, & Costantini, 2013) and cognitions about God (Saide & Richert, 2020) and prayer (Bamford & Lagattuta, 2010), findings elaborated in the section on social and cognitive developmental research.

Stearns and McKinney (2019a) also found considerable variation in whether and for whom the intergenerational transference of RS occurred. Although relatively few studies have replicated moderators that could account for the heterogeneity in effect sizes, Stearns and McKinney (2019a) were able tease apart the direct and interactive effects of parent and youth gender on the strength of covariation between parental and adolescent RS. Specifically, the transmission effect was stronger for mothers relative to fathers across adolescent gender (fifteen studies), for sons relative to daughters across parental gender (six studies), and within mother-daughter dyads compared to the other three combinations of parent-adolescent gender based on studies with sufficient details for these comparisons (five studies).

Parenting mechanisms of RS socialization. A positive parent-youth relationship is another key family factor that facilitates RS across generations (Stearns & McKinney, 2019b). For instance, warm and supportive parent-youth relationships heighten the likelihood that US adolescents (Hardy, White, Zhang, & Ruchty, 2011) and Indonesian Muslim youth (French, Eisenberg, Sallquist, Purwono, Lu, & Christ, 2013) adopt their parents' level of RS. In addition, among African American households, higher authoritative parenting style in general combined with higher parental RS have been found to predict unique variance in youths' own RS for late adolescents and college students, with no main effects of parenting style or parental RS in this study (Abar, Carter, & Winsler, 2009). In addition, adults' memories of a secure attachment history with caregivers as well as current secure attachment have been linked to a higher degree of parent-offspring similarity in many aspects of RS (Granqvist & Kirkpatrick, 2013). Multiple studies using older data sets likewise suggest that better parent-adolescent relationship dynamics enhance the intergenerational transmission of RS (see Hardy et al., 2019; Smith & Adamczyk, 2021). In summary, parental sensitivity and warmth may powerfully shape children's RS development, although studies are needed that incorporate children's self-reports of RS and parenting, along with direct observation of parenting.

Polarization in parental transmission of RS and non-RS. It is important to recognize that the intergenerational transmission of RS increasingly reflects the transmission of both RS engagement and disengagement, at least in the United States. Two in-depth longitudinal studies of largely working-class families from California address this point. First, Bengtson, Hayward, Zuckerman, and Silverstein (2018) argued that a near tripling of nonreligious youth from 1971 to 2005 reflects parents transmitting either a RS or non-RS heritage, rather than merely failed efforts by more RS parents to foster higher RS in their offspring. For instance, the authors found that the dramatic rise of young adults who endorsed being nonreligious was tied to their parents becoming less engaged in RS across the thirty-four-year period. In addition, an increasing number of two-parent families included one parent who was nonreligious, a situation that increased the odds that youth would even more rapidly disassociate compared to having two religiously affiliated parents. Second, Bengtson, Copen, Putney, and Silverstein (2009) found that from 1970 to 2000 the influence of grandparents on their adult grandchildren's RS had significantly weakened, including service attendance at any place of worship and general religious commitment. An opposite pattern occurred for conservative religious beliefs where there was a significant grandparent-to-grandchild transmission effect in 2000, but not in 1971. These contrasting patterns may reflect growing polarization by US parents, who are both more and less RS, in shaping their offspring's adoption of (non)RS as a foundation for daily life (Bengtson et al., 2018).

Parental polarization in the United States of RS socialization being a (non) priority for child-rearing is also vividly illustrated by analyses that Smith and

Adamczyk (2021) conducted on data from a 2010 Culture of American Families Survey (CAFS; Institute for Advanced Studies in Culture, 2012). This nationally representative survey is unique for its in-depth focus on the role of RS for parenting based on responses of parents ($N = 2,904$) who had at least one child (ages 5–18) living at home, not just adolescents. Specifically, 34 percent of parents said their top personal goal in parenting was to rear children "whose lives reflect God's will and purpose" whereas 31 percent ranked this goal as dead last, and the other 35 percent ranked this priority somewhere in the middle. The other four goals included nurture children's positive self-regard and interpersonal relationships; rear children who contribute to their communities and the world; rear children who adhere to their family roots and cultural traditions; and provide material or educational resources to optimize children achieving their life goals. As another indicator of the limited centrality of RS for parenting, only 29 percent of US parents rated rearing children of strong religious faith as essential or very important, with 71 percent saying this goal was not very important. On the other end of the continuum, parental worries that their children may lose their RS faith was "only a small concern" for 23 percent of parents and not a concern at all for 44 percent, with this fear ranking well below others (e.g., serious accidents, addictions, lack of ambition, financial failure). Thus, a minority of US parents appear to be strongly motivated to transmit a high level of RS to their children. Similar data are needed from other countries.

Parental RS mechanisms of RS socialization. Researchers have attempted to quantify which parental RS factors most contribute to adolescents' RS socialization. Religious affiliation per se is unimportant, even among families involved in more conservative groups net of other RS variables (Smith & Adamczyk, 2021). Instead, a key RS ingredient that directly predicts offspring RS are a given parent's own importance of faith and religious service attendance, along with the congruence between these two individual factors (Bader & Desmond, 2006). Similarity between married parents' RS attendance and subjective importance of RS also heightens adolescent RS (McPhail, 2019). In addition, supportive youth-parent dialogues about RS are tied to greater adolescent RS (Desrosiers, Kelly, & Miller, 2011; King, Furrow, & Roth, 2002). Finally, highly RS parents "channel" their teens toward forming close connections to RS communities and peers, additional RS social factors tied to adolescent RS (Pearce & Denton, 2011).

Notably, Smith and Adamczyk (2021) found that only 35 percent of US parents think that they should lead their children and adolescents to accept the parents' faith with 65 percent believing youth should be led to decide their RS views on their own. The former group mirrors the minority of US parents who are highly devout, including those who attend religious services weekly (35 percent) and rate religious faith as the "very most important thing in life" (17 percent). Nearly all of these very devout parents say they talk with their children about religious topics and take their children to religious services at least weekly. By contrast, few other parents engage in such behavior. Stepping back, most US youth spend limited time engaged in home or institutionally based RS activities compared to many other pursuits (e.g., school, sports, internet/media consumption), and most US parents invest limited effort in key RS mechanisms that would facilitate their children's RS development.

Qualitative Evidence on Intergenerational Transmission of RS

A rich array of qualitative studies has recruited parents actively involved in RS communities to solicit parents' thoughts about their role in transmitting RS beliefs and practices to their children. The most relevant project for this Element was completed by Smith, Ritz, and Rotolo (2019), who conducted 215 in-depth interviews in 2014 and 2015 with US parents who had at least one child between ages five and eighteen in residence. These parents were purposely selected because they belonged to various Christian, conservative Jewish, Mormon, Muslim, Hindu, and Buddhist groups and reported either very high (63 percent) or low (27 percent) involvement in their RS community. Most participants were married to the opposite-sex parent of their child (63 percent), with a minority being remarried (17 percent), single (17 percent), or in a same-sex union (3 percent). Extensive descriptions of these qualitative interviews are available in Smith et al. (2019) and in Smith and Adamczyk (2021) that integrate the project's qualitative themes with quantitative findings. Smith and colleagues (Smith & Adamczyk, 2021; Smith et al., 2019) had originally expected to uncover robust and complex differences stemming from diverse RS traditions. However, these US parents' comments largely converged as to why and how they should pass on their RS beliefs and practices to their children. In a nutshell, parents agreed:

> Parents are responsible for preparing their children for the challenging journey of life, during which they will hopefully become their best possible selves and live happy, good lives. Religion provides crucial help for navigating life's journey successfully, including moral guidance, emotional support, and a secure home base. So parents should equip their children with knowledge of their religion by routinely modeling its practices, values, and ethics, which children will then hopefully absorb and embrace for themselves. (Smith & Admaczyk, 2021, p. 12)

Furthermore, nearly all of the religiously engaged parents shared what Smith and Admaczyk (2021) identified as the dominant US cultural view that the primary purpose of life is to:

> [L]ead a happy and good life, in the dual sense of both having life go well (enjoying success and happiness) and living life rightly (doing what is morally right). A good life is one in which self-directed individuals are happy, live ethically, work hard, enjoy family and friends, and help other people. Good lives must be self-determined and pursued in ways that are true to each unique individual self. But they should not be individualistic in the sense of isolated or selfish; they must always be realized and enjoyed with others, in and with communities, groups, families, and probably marriage partners. Good lives achieve a certain quality of life in this world, in the here and now; they are not primarily preparing for the hereafter, eternity, or some ultimate reality. (p. 14)

Another clear consensus of most parents was that life's journey involves certain challenges:

> The world, which exists beyond the walls of the family home, "out there," offers potential for growth, achievement, and fulfillment, but also threats of instability, confusion, danger, and failure. The world presents a variety of paths to travel and options to choose – some good, some bad. "The culture" sends some bad "messages" that, if believed, threaten success on life's journey, which therefore must be recognized and resisted. Even when life's journey goes well, everyone faces trials, makes mistakes, and confronts discouragement along the way; but these can be overcome when one is properly equipped with resources to surmount them. (p. 16)

In short, parents actively engaged in diverse RS communities believed their children needed to have a firm sense of self that is rooted in the parents' RS beliefs as a pathway to become self-actualized, happy, and good people and avoid getting lost in the journey of life. The parents generally were *not* concerned about their children learning the particular doctrinal claims or teachings of a given religious tradition. Rather, parents generally thought that all or most religious traditions seek the truth, and children need to learn two critical religious truths: one vaguely theological and existential; one instrumental and functional, as follows:

> First, children should learn to "believe in something" along the lines that "there is a greater picture" out there, "something bigger" going on, such as a God who is with us and answers prayers or the force of karma. Second, religion can help people live good lives in this world. However, exclusivity, superiority, and fanaticism in religions are bad, dangerous, and must be avoided. Even if one believes that no one religion has a monopoly on truth,

it is still not a bad idea to belong to some particular religious tradition or community, to be located somewhere specific. Beyond the two paramount truths, however, one can take from one's own religious tradition the parts that make sense and work best, and leave the parts that don't, according to "whatever seems right" to you. (p. 20)

Consistent with other qualitative interviews with married heterosexuals highly engaged in monotheistic religious traditions (Barrow, Dollahite, & Marks, 2020), many RS parents felt they faced a difficult quandary; they wanted to instill these two truths yet also avoid violating their children's self-determination and triggering teenage rebellion by being excessively pushy. In navigating this line, Smith and Admaczyk (2021) observed that even conservative RS parents generally subjugated their RS tradition's dictates, as needed, to sustain family harmony. Shared RS beliefs and practices were thought to foster family solidarity but were jettisoned if they interfered with other bonding activities (e.g., sports). Also, parents did not anticipate a child switching to or marrying someone from a different RS tradition as problematic as long as the child followed the two basic religious truths.

The main mechanisms parents said they used to transmit their faith were to live out their personal RS beliefs diligently and without hypocrisy and be a role model for RS practices (e.g., prayer, worship services, volunteering). By "walking the walk," parents believed children would passively absorb the value of RS by observation. Most parents avoided initiating RS discussions for fear of coming across as religiously dogmatic or coercive. Parents also did not express a sense of responsibility, or even the capability, of explaining the orthodox content of their RS tradition to their children and they only occasionally proactively disclosed their private RS ideas or experiences. Although most felt they needed to take younger children to religious services or activities, they generally stepped aside to allow their teens to make their own RS decisions. Parents saw themselves, and not religious communities, as being in charge of their children's RS development, and none emphasized their children needing a conversion or "religious experience." In summary, parents expressed confidence in their own ability to pass along their approach to RS to their children, along with some help from God and flexible access to religious congregations. As a reminder, this study disproportionally selected parents (63 percent) who reported very high involvement across diverse RS communities.

Numerous qualitative studies echo and extend Smith and Adamczyk's (2021) observations to subsets of US (e.g., Dollahite, Marks, Babcock, Barrow, & Rose, 2019) and Irish (e.g., Kelley, Galbraith & Korth, 2020) families composed of married heterosexuals with teens who are highly engaged in their organized religious group. Qualitative studies of families who do not fit this "traditional" family structure promoted by most religious institutions yield similar themes. For example, Sullivan (2011) offered poignant findings on single and economically disadvantaged mothers in US cities. Despite often feeling stigmatized by organized religious groups due to being unmarried, many of these solo mothers nevertheless strived for their children to internalize a sense of connection to God/higher power and get involved in a particular religious community to ensure their psychosocial and RS well-being. Similarly, in a unique qualitative study of families headed by same-sex couples who reported past RS struggles with others, parents often engaged in child-centered dialogues about RS and worked to provide their children with a sense of belonging to a welcoming RS community and connection to a higher power (Rostosky, Abreu, Mahoney, & Riggle, 2017).

Reciprocal Influence of Children on Parental RS

Although social scientists emphasize the downward impact of parents shaping their children's (non)RS beliefs or behaviors, reverse generational influences also occur. That is, children can reciprocally impact their parents' RS over the lifespan (Bengtson et al., 2013; King & Boyatzis, 2015). This process starts when adults become parents. Specifically, some people who fall away from participation in organized religious groups in early adulthood return after they have children. This pattern, however, primarily occurs for the minority of adults who were very actively engaged in RS as teens. For example, according to longitudinal data, both married and single US parents who attended religious services weekly as adolescents, but disengaged during early adulthood, are much more likely to return to a religious institution after they have children compared to their childless single counterparts (Uecker, Mayrl, & Stroope, 2016). However, adults who were minimally involved in religious groups as adolescents did not join religious groups after marriage or having children (Schleifer & Chaves, 2017). Also, for couples, it is becoming co-parents that facilitates reintegration into religious groups rather than tying the marital knot (Gurrentz, 2017). Thus, unlike childfree adults, the high stakes of rearing a family may lead both married and unmarried parents with a RS upbringing to reach out to RS communities for support to socialize their children.

Children's comments or questions about RS can also prompt parental RS growth. For instance, Boyatzis and Janicki (2003) collected mixed-methods data from Christian two-parent families ($N = 23$ with children ages 3 to 12 from a semirural area of the United States) where mothers recorded in a diary every conversation they had with their children about RS over a two-week span. These mothers and children discussed RS issues nearly three times per week with the most common topics being God, Jesus, and prayer. Children initiated and terminated about half the conversations, spoke as much as parents did, and frequently asked questions and offered their own views. In short, parent-child communication about RS was bidirectional and appeared to deepen parents' reflections about their own RS identities. Qualitative researchers have also begun to note that parents and children influence each other's' RS lives (Dollahite et al., 2019). Finally, employing their longitudinal data set discussed earlier and utilizing the life course perspective concept of "linked lives," Bengtson et al. (2013) illustrated that children and parents influence one another's RS identities over the lifespan.

Summary on RS Intergenerational Transmission Findings

Taken together, research with US parents of adolescents and young adults indicates that parents play a powerful role in whether youth adopt RS as part of their own identity. Yet, based on recent quantitative evidence, only around a third of US parents identify their offspring's RS development as a major priority of parenting. Furthermore, US parents who are more highly engaged in an organized religious community view themselves as the primary party responsible for facilitating their children's RS development, not their religious communities or authority figures. These parents' central hopes appear to be that their children will develop a firm sense of connection with "something bigger" than the self to help them become well-functioning adults, while at the same time avoiding being intolerant of others' RS identities. Scarce empirical research exists on parents' views of their roles in shaping their children's receptivity to RS outside the US cultural context. Very limited attention within RS intergenerational transmission literature has targeted families with children under the age of 12, although the following section of this Element highlights mixed evidence that parental socialization processes contribute to young children's cognitions about God.

Social and Cognitive-Developmental Research on Children's RS Development

According to Boyatzis (2013), initial empirical research on children's cognitions about RS focused on integrating Piagetian models of cognitive development with RS concepts, particularly concepts of God. By the 1990s, the dominant position of cognitive scientists was that children's RS cognitions operate under the same principles of theory of mind, agency, and mental-physical causality that apply to other cognitive domains. This section of the Element summarizes related findings but begins by discussing the intersection of attachment theory and children's RS cognitions because distinctions are made in the literature between peoples' understanding of *God image* versus *God concept*. God image refers to individuals' internal working mental model and emotional experiences of God as an attachment figure, whereas God concept refers to theological knowledge involving cognitions about God, prayer, and the afterlife (Davis, Moriarty, & Mauch, 2013). Although the God image and God concept constructs overlap, each has generated its own body of science.

God Image and Attachment Theory

Theory and evidence based on studies of adolescents and adults. Extending attachment theory to children's RS development, Kirkpatrick proposed that humans' experiential understanding of God is based on their internal working models (IWMs) derived from interpersonal interactions (Granqvist, 2020; Granqvist & Kirkpatrick, 2013). According to Granqvist (2020), evidence indicates that IWMs reflect internalized schemas about the extent to which other people are experienced as consistently available and responsive as well as whether the self is experienced as worthy of love, care, and esteem. IWMs initially develop through early experiences with caregivers, but subsequent interactions with attachment figures throughout the lifespan can revise IWMs. Kirkpatrick offered two hypotheses for how God images can come to reflect children's (and adults') IWMs. First, the correspondence hypothesis contends that children who experience their primary caregivers as caring and trustworthy will similarly experience God as a secure attachment figure. Empirically, associations exist between adults' recollections of secure attachment histories and current reports of having secure attachment styles with adults viewing God as a secure attachment object (Davis, Granqvist, & Sharp, 2018; Granqvist, 2020; Granqvist & Kirkpatrick, 2013). Alternatively, Kirkpatrick's compensatory hypothesis proposes that children who are chronically exposed to inconsistent, harsh, or neglectful caregivers could turn to God as a surrogate secure attachment figure, assuming they are exposed to other influences (e.g., RS teachings or mentors) that help them develop an image of God as a safe, caring, and responsive divine being. Children could then rely on a felt secure attachment to God to regulate emotional distress they experience in human relationships. Empirical studies with adults offer support for the compensation hypothesis. Specifically, adults with insecure attachment histories are more likely to have sudden religious conversions, especially during times of loss or distress in their human relationships (Granqvist, 2020). Also, adolescents and adults benefit from psychologically turning to a loving God figure for comfort and support to cope with difficulties (Davis et al., 2018; Granqvist, 2020;

Granqvist & Kirkpatrick, 2013). Yet, only four peer-reviewed studies have directly examined links between children's perceptions of their felt relationships with parents and God.

Evidence based on studies of children. In an initial promising effort in 1997, Dickie et al. asked two US samples of 4- to 11-year-olds to rate their parents' and God's nurturance and strength: (1) forty-nine Caucasian children with married parents from middle-upper-class backgrounds, recruited from a local Protestant church, and (2) ninety-four children from lower-middle-class backgrounds with more ethnic diversity, recruited from local public pre/schools (geographic region not indicated). Within both groups, robust associations emerged between children's perceptions of parents and God being nurturing and strong, especially when mothers were perceived as powerful and fathers were perceived as nurturing. However, children whose parents used more punitive discipline strategies viewed God as less nurturing or powerful. Finally, children's ratings of God as nurturing and strong increased with child age as well as in homes without fathers. Overall, these findings imply that children's secure attachment to God mirrors positive parent-child relationships and could function as a substitute attachment figure as children grow less dependent on parents.

In another innovative study, 5- to 7-year-old Swedish children ($N = 40$, recruited equally from Christian groups and secular schools) completed a structured separation anxiety interview to assess their attachment status (Granqvist, Ljungdahl, & Dickie, 2007). They also listened to stories about visually represented children in attachment-activating and attachment-neutral situations and then placed a God symbol on a felt board to represent God's closeness to the fictional children. Children's God's closeness was greater in attachment-activating situations, particularly for securely attached children; this supports a hypothesis of IWM correspondence between the children's models of self-others and God. Higher parents' RS did not moderate these links, but was correlated with God's closeness. In another study using a similar storytelling methodology with Italian 6- to 8-year-olds ($N = 71$), the attachment pattern of children's mothers (not the children) was assessed (Cassiba et al., 2013). Children of secure mothers placed the God symbol closer than children of insecure mothers across both types of situations, implying that mother-child interactions may shape children's closeness to God. In addition, girls, but not boys, placed the God symbol closer in attachment-activating than in attachment-neutral situations, partially supporting the God-as-safe-haven model found in Granqvist et al. (2007). Contrary to expectations, however, neither mothers' global RS nor their attachment to God was directly correlated with children's closeness to God.

Finally, De Roos, Miedema, and Iedema (2001) assessed Dutch kindergar-
teners' ($N = 72$, recruited equally from a Protestant and public school) attachment to their mother, quality of relationships with teacher and peers, and
perceptions of God as loving or punishing using various structured methods.
Contrary to expectations, children's perceived attachment to their mothers was
unrelated to their perceptions of God, possibly because most children (65 percent) lived in nonreligious homes. However, children's reports of greater
harmony and closeness in teacher-child relationships and more acceptance by
peers were both tied to a loving God concept, perhaps because most children
(79 percent) received religious education from their teacher whom the children
then associated with a positive God image. Null results emerged for children's
perceptions of a punishing God concept.

Summary of empirical studies on God image and children. Attachment theory
offers a well-known theoretical foundation for examining the development of
children's bonds with God or other supernatural figures. More studies with
children as participants are needed to consistently establish and better elucidate
how children's attachments to adults predict their felt attachment to God and
what adaptive functions either a corresponding or compensatory attachment to
God play for children.

God Concepts

As summarized by Boyatzis (2013), research conducted prior to the 1990s
found that children's drawings generally reflected anthropomorphic images of
God, although variation emerged depending on children's religious tradition.
Children from Christian families generated the most anthropomorphic portrayals, whereas children with Jewish backgrounds rendered images that were
more abstract, and those with Hindu backgrounds drew multifaceted images.
Such research seemed consistent with Piaget's premise that youth cannot
comprehend more abstract concepts about God until they pass out of the
cognitive stage of concrete operations, perhaps no sooner than early adolescence. However, at least seventeen peer-reviewed studies published since 2000
indicate that preschool- and elementary-aged children often attribute supernatural qualities to God (e.g., omniscience, immortality), even after recognizing
humans are fallible and mortal. The Element now delves into these studies.

Children's Cognitions about God

Born believers? Barrett, Richert, and Driesenga (2001) suggested that preschoolers can distinguish a deity's supernatural abilities from human limitations
using US samples of 2- to 7-year-old children ($N = 24$, New York; $N = 52$,

Michigan; $N = 45$, Michigan) reared in Protestant families. In two false belief experiments, children were shown a closed saltine cracker box that contained rocks, not crackers. Most 3- and 4-year-olds said that God, their mother, a bear, an ant, or a tree would know there were rocks in the box despite appearances to the contrary. By contrast, most 5- and 6-year-olds reported that only God would be omniscient, and the other parties would falsely look inside the box to get crackers. Similarly, in a third appearance-reality task, children were shown a block hidden inside of a box, and then asked if God, a monkey puppet, a girl puppet, or a kitty that could see in the dark would detect the hidden object in the darkened box. The younger children indicated that all parties could do this without illumination. By contrast, the older children indicated that only God and the special kitty would detect the hidden object. Extending these findings, Barrett, Newman, and Richert (2003) recruited 3- to 7-year-old children ($N = 51$) with Christian backgrounds from California and Michigan. They presented the children with partial and then complete visual information about a hidden picture, secret written code, and novel game with geometrical shapes. After the 3- and 4-year-olds were given all visual information, most claimed their mother and God would understand what the partial visual displays meant even in the absence of sufficient information. By contrast, both before and after possessing complete visual information, all of the 5- to 7-year-olds said that God would understand the unrecognizable displays, with small minorities saying this about their mother or dog. In another study, Richert and Barrett (2005) recruited 3- to 7-year-old children ($N = 39$) from Protestant churches in Michigan and exposed them to visual, auditory, and olfactory stimuli that they could not detect from a distance but could identify on closer inspection. The children were then asked about God's ability to detect the inaccessible sensory stimuli, along with five puppets including an eagle with special sight, a fox with special hearing, a dog with special smelling abilities, a normal monkey, and a girl. All of the children reported that God and each special animal with the relevant sensory advantage would have greater perceptual abilities to see, hear, or smell the stimuli compared to humans and normal animals with limited sensory abilities. Also, the children's views of God and the special being's extraordinary powers remained stable across ages, while older children further downgraded the sensory abilities of the other characters. Finally, Burdett and Barrett (2016) recruited 3- to 5-year-old children from Israeli Modern Orthodox Jewish families ($N = 64$) and from UK families, most of whom (82 percent) attended an Anglican church ($N = 76$). According to the authors, all age groups regarded God as more unconstrained from biological life-cycle properties than humans, with children's accurate recognition of theological differences increasing from age three to five.

Taken together, Barrett and colleagues' studies with young children reared in Christian or Jewish homes suggested that many 3- and 4-year-old children could report theologically correct perceptions of God having omniscient powers and sustain these perceptions from age five onward after increasingly realizing that human minds can hold false beliefs (Barrett & Richert, 2003; Richert & Smith, 2009). Notably, developing an accurate "representational understanding" of human minds as being fallible unfolds across childhood, with about 50 percent of 4- to 5-year-olds and nearly 100 percent of 8- to 9-year-olds passing standard false belief tasks (Burdett & Barrett, 2016). One interpretation of the body of work on children's cognitions of God discussed thus far has been that human beings have evolved to be "naturally" cognitively prepared very early in life to acquire beliefs that deities possess supernatural characteristics that are counter-intuitive and distinctive from abilities possessed by human agents (Barrett, 2012; Richert & Smith, 2009; Shook, 2017).

Persistent believers? The studies discussed next have found that children must be at least five years old to correctly differentiate God's supernatural abilities from humans' fallible perceptual abilities, and then persist in holding such beliefs. These studies raise doubts as to whether young children mentally represent God's properties as qualitatively distinct from egocentrism and anthropomorphism. Instead, these studies indicate that children continue to attribute supernatural powers to God as they age due to ongoing RS socialization processes (Lane et al., 2010; Lane, Wellman, & Evans, 2012).

Attempting to replicate and extend Barrett and colleagues' work, Giménez-Dasí, Guerrero, and Harris (2005) interviewed 3-, 4-, and 5-year-olds from Spain (total $N = 72$) and examined differences in their perceptions of the immortality and omniscience of their best friend compared to God. In responding to focused-choice questions, the 3- and 4-year-olds reported that both parties would have false beliefs about the contents of a candy box filled with pencils (i.e., not be omniscient) and be equally constrained by biological processes of birth, growth, and death. Only the 5-year-olds endorsed the theologically correct belief that God would not fall prey to false beliefs and was unconstrained by the human life cycle. Makris and Pnevmatikos (2007) used methodologies similar to Barrett et al. (2001) with 3- to 7-year-old children ($N = 127$) from Greek Orthodox middle-class families and also found that children had to be around five years old to generate a clear understanding of a supernatural mind. For example, around 75 percent of 3- and 4-year-olds reported that God as well as the mother had no knowledge about the content of the closed box. Thus, most of these preschoolers did not attribute omniscience to God but saw God as having the limitations of human minds. Also, Lane et al. (2010) recruited three age groups (40 to 49.4 months, 49.5 to 54.5 months, and 54.5 to 59 months) of

Christian US children and examined children's attributions of false beliefs to their mother and the following characters: a girl, a special cat and superhero with abnormal visual powers, an all-knowing man, and God. Different age-related trends emerged depending on the target agent: (1) an increasing linear trend to attribute psychologically correct fallible mental states to the human girl and mom; (2) a constant trend to attribute superior mental abilities to the special cat and superhero; and (3) a curvilinear trend where children first increasingly attributed fallible human mental states to God and the omniscient man from ages 40 to 50 months, but by 55+ months assigned correct superpowers (i.e., omniscience) to those two agents.

Additional evidence suggests young children are taught to maintain God's supernatural status after realizing humans are fallible, rather than understanding as preschoolers that God is qualitatively different from humans. When attempting to replicate Barrett et al. (2001) among 4- to 7-year-old Mayan Catholic children ($N = 48$), for example, Knight, Sousa, Barrett, and Atran (2004) found that only children age six and older only reliably passed the false belief task (a year later than typically found for US children). Parallel to the curvilinear pattern in Lane et al., the Mayan children increasingly reported fallible human mental states to God and the parent from age five to six, but by age seven God had returned to prior levels of infallibility. Also, Lane et al. (2012) replicated that only 5-year-olds differentiated between humans' fallible minds and God's less fallible mind among another sample of US Christian 3- to 5-year-olds ($N = 61$) using various theory-of-mind tasks. Moreover, unlike secularly schooled children, religiously schooled 4-year-olds appreciated another non-human agent's less fallible mental abilities after being instructed and reminded about those special abilities. Furthermore, Kiessling and Perner (2014) examined Austrian 3- to 6-year-olds ($N = 100$) attending Catholic schools and compared children's explanations of whether and how they, as well as God, and a baby and mother puppet would detect contents hidden inside a box across eight trials. Younger (prerepresentational) children attributed their own reality assessment (i.e., egocentrism) to all three agents. Of children mastering the task of seeing humans as fallible (representational), younger children largely conceived God as an ignorant "man in the sky" and then God was increasingly viewed by older children as a "supernatural agent in the sky," presumably due to more RS education or training.

Children's RS affiliation and broad cultural factors. Other studies have further addressed ways that broad RS sociocultural factors may influence children's reasoning about ordinary and extraordinary minds by expanding studies beyond children being reared in Western cultural contexts. For example, Burdett, Wigger, and Barrett (2019) gave a knowledge-ignorance theory-of-mind task to 3- to 5-year-olds from active Protestant families from the United Kingdom ($N = 71$), Dominican Republic ($N = 51$), Kenya ($N = 57$), and Modern Orthodox Jewish families from Israel ($N = 64$). A very complex pattern of between- and within-group findings emerged that suggested broader cultural forces play salient roles in shaping Protestant Christian children's understandings of various extraordinary minds, including God, angels, ancestors, and Swec (an unfamiliar name children were told belonged to a person with superpowers and the ability to see through things). Burdett, Barrett, and Greenway (2020) recruited 2- to 5-year-old children from the United Kingdom ($N = 76$), Albania ($N = 60$), and Israel ($N = 60$), respectively, from families from Christian, Muslim, and Jewish backgrounds. Children completed two perception (audio and visual) tasks and one memory task to assess their understanding of natural and supernatural minds' cognitive abilities. Although different patterns emerged for children's responses about human minds based on their RS tradition, their convergent responses about God suggest that children from religious traditions with a "High God" (God, Allah, Ha-Shem) understand theistic concepts similarly. Nyhof and Johnson (2017) examined 3- to 7-year-olds from Latter-Day-Saints and mainstream Protestant families in the United States as well as Indonesian children from Muslim and Catholic families with several theory-of-mind tasks. Regardless of type of religious affiliation, the youngest children similarly distinguished God from humans. Older children's conceptions of God, however, were more congruent with the distinct theological teachings of their traditions. Also, all children generally attributed more omniscience rather than omnipresence to God, perhaps because the latter theological concept is more difficult to grasp until older ages.

Parental RS and children's RS activity. Other theory-of-mind experiments with US children have focused on the extent to which parental or child RS activity (e.g., frequency of public and private RS activities, formal RS education) and affiliation each contribute to children differentiating God from humans. Although children's overall RS activity was not uniquely related to their God concepts, Richert, Saide, Lesage, and Shaman (2017) found that preschoolers from Muslim families were more likely to view human minds as being more fallible than God's than preschoolers from Protestant, Catholic, and religiously nonaffiliated families ($N = 272$, California). Also, the 3- to 5-year-olds who most differentiated between human and God's minds had parents who themselves held the least anthropomorphic conceptions of God. Conversely, the children from families who were not religiously affiliated were the least likely to report differences between the minds of humans and God. In a similarly diverse RS sample ($N = 215$, California), Saide and Richert (2020) unexpectedly found that 3- to 7-year-olds' views of God as having human characteristics (e.g., has a heart, eats/drinks, gets sick or bored) were unrelated to the frequency of their own RS practices or parents' concept of God after controlling for the child's age. Children also viewed God as being more anthropomorphic than their parents, especially younger children; however, children agreed more with their parents' concepts of God as nonhuman when the child's sociocognitive reasoning skills were more advanced. Finally, in a study of children's false belief inferences about popular occult characters along with God, Lam and Guerrero (2020) recruited 5- to 10-year-olds from Spain ($N = 72$) and England ($N = 76$) from secular settings, although most of the latter children belonged to Muslim families. Children were asked if three humans (mother, classmate, teacher), three animals (dog, bear, bird), and three supernatural beings (Superman, fairy, God) could detect whether and why rocks, not candy, were inside a candy box. Across both countries, most children reported that humans would have false beliefs, whereas God would be more likely than other agents to hold correct beliefs. However, British children with more religiously active parents, and especially Muslims, were more likely than nonaffiliates to see God as omniscient due to God's having extraordinary powers (data were not collected about the Spanish children's level of RS engagement).

Prayer

Although only two quantitative peer-reviewed studies appear to have examined children's subjective experiences of prayer prior to 2010 (Long, Elkind, & Spilka, 1967; Woolley & Phelps, 2001), several studies conducted since then offer fascinating insights into contemporary US children's understanding of prayer. Bamford and Lagattuta (2010) recruited college students ($N = 40$) as well as 4-, 6-, and 8-year-old children ($N = 60$) from the US Pacific Northwest, with children's parents identifying as Christian (71 percent), nonaffiliated (15 percent), or non-Christian (13 percent). The researchers used multiple vignettes to probe children's cognitions about the nature of prayer, how the characters' emotions might trigger prayer, and how prayer might influence coping with emotions. By age six or eight, children better understood that prayer is a mental activity done in one's head that involves talking to God, whereas nearly all 4-year-olds offered superficial or rote explanations about what prayer was. For emotional functioning, the two younger age groups believed that positive emotions would cause people to pray more than negative emotions. By age eight, children believed that negative rather than positive emotions would trigger prayer. As children got older, they also realized that prayers of thanksgiving were more relevant for positive versus negative situations. Regarding coping, 4-year-old children tended to focus on characters feeling better after praying, especially in the context of positive events, whereas older children thought characters would feel better from praying in a sad or scary situation. Finally, few consistent linkages emerged between children's understandings of prayer and their parents' prayer life or other RS activities (e.g., worship attendance, parent-child RS discussions); these results raise questions about whether general cognitive maturation or RS socialization most fosters children's beliefs about prayer.

Using a series of vignettes, Lane, Evans, Brink, and Wellman (2016) examined how 3- to 10-year-old children and adults ($N = 183$) conceive of communication with humans versus God. Participants were given scenarios in which a protagonist wanted help from a parent or from God. Variations were based on whether protagonists expressed their desires aloud (by asking) or silently (by hoping), whether parents or God were nearby or far away in each story, and whether protagonists expressed their desires through ordinary communication (asking or hoping) or more extraordinary means (praying). Following each scenario, participants were asked whether either the parent or God was aware of the protagonist's desire. Children as young as 3- to 4-years-old understood that both loudness and distance limit the effectiveness of human communication, saying that humans would most likely be aware of desires when they were expressed both aloud and nearby. By this age, children also reported that God would more often be aware of desires than would humans. Children of all ages often reported that God, like humans, would be more aware of desires expressed aloud rather than silently. These concepts of communication via prayer to God or ordinary communication with humans continued to be refined through middle childhood. Children's better performance on standard theory-of-mind tasks and greater RS background also predicted whether they attributed awareness to God.

Following up on these two investigations, Lane (2020) addressed differences in 3- to 11-year-olds' ($N = 144$) and college students' ($N = 85$) predictions about the fulfillment of prayers and wishes. Specifically, Lane examined whether the children's and adults' predictions about the occurrence of desired outcomes differed due to their desires being expressed as wishes versus prayers, being plausible versus impossible, and their religious backgrounds. Participants were read scenarios where the protagonist either wished or prayed for a desired event to occur. Some of the desired events could plausibly happen with ordinary human intervention, and others were impossible, even with human intervention. Preschoolers often predicted that desired outcomes would occur, but with increasing age, participants judged that fewer events would occur. Across the entire age range, participants recognized that impossible events would be obtained less often than plausible events, indicating that common-sense probabilistic reasoning lessened expectations about God fulfilling supernatural petitions. For both children and adults, greater RS experiences increased their expectations that prayers, but not wishes, would result in desired outcomes.

Two studies have examined children's and their parents' understanding of specific physical actions often ritualistically associated with prayer (e.g., bent head, closed eyes, kneeling) and the mental state of God. Shaman, Saide, Lesage, and Richert (2016) interviewed preschool children (ages 3 to 7) and one parent ($N = 182$) from Protestant, Catholic, and Muslim backgrounds. After controlling for age and their parents' views about prayer, children tended to report that the overt behavioral aspects of prayer signaled to other people the nature of the private communication with God, but God does not need such signals to hear prayers. Thus, children's belief that prayer requires specific overt actions related to children's perceptions of the limitations of human minds rather than God's knowledge. In addition, children who believed that prayer should not include unconventional actions (e.g., standing on one's head) had parents who also advocated this view, suggesting that children's beliefs about ritualistically correct ways to pray reflect the messages they receive from their parents. Expanding their investigation to 246 mother-child dyads, Richert, Shaman, Saide, and Lesage (2016) found that both parties primarily believe that the overt behavioral actions of prayer help the individual praying to think about God. In addition, parents who endorsed the possibility that ritualistic prayer actions served a communicative function to connect with God had children with more anthropomorphic views of God.

Summary of empirical studies on children's God concepts and prayer. Since the early 2000s, cognitive-developmental researchers have tackled the challenge of conducting scientific inquiry into children's attachment to God and cognitive understanding of God and prayer. Available findings illustrate that such cognitions are amendable to cognitive-developmental research methods rather than waiting for children to reach preadolescence or adolescence. Namely, as early as age three, children sometimes report God as possessing supernatural abilities, although such perceptions tend to solidify in theological accuracy and be differentiated from children's understanding that humans are fallible after age five or six. By around age six, children often also report turning to God for help or comfort in prayer. Such perceptions tend to align with the family RS context in which children are reared and substantive RS messages they may receive about the nature of God or prayer, especially from their parents. Yet largely null findings have emerged as linkages between children's concepts of God and children or parents' greater engagement in organized religious activities per se, underscoring once again the role that parents appear to play as gatekeepers in directly or indirectly shaping their children's RS development, intentionally or unintentionally.

Notably, cognitive-developmental research on young children's cognitions about God's supernatural abilities has contributed to ongoing debate between philosophers and scientists about the "preparedness hypothesis." This premise posits that humans have evolved to be innately predisposed to believe in and pray to supernatural agents across the lifespan (i.e., "born believers") rather than merely being acculturated to believe in and relate to such entities (Rickert & Smith, 2009). It is well beyond the scope of this Element to adjudicate continuing contentious discussions about how and why humans of all ages have acquired, maintained, transformed, and transmitted RS concepts over the course of evolutionary history. This debate also draws on a handful of studies not reviewed in this Element on children's and adults' coexisting supernatural and natural explanations of various events (e.g., origins of species, illness, death) and acceptance of counterintuitive testimony (e.g., Legare, Evans, Rosengren, & Harris, 2012). Illustrative insights into this debate can be found in a special section of *Method & Theory in the Study of Religion* with a lead article by Shook (2017), along with rebuttals, as well as an Element focused on this topic by De Smedt and De Cruz (2020).

Further Directions for Cognitive-Developmental Research on Children

This Element's review of social and cognitive-developmental studies on children's RS cognitions converges with Richert and Smith's observations (2009) of this literature. Namely, researchers have only begun to identify cognitive and social factors that set the stage for children's experiential and cognitive understandings of God and felt communication with God (i.e., prayer). Especially after age five or six, young children often report that God, but not humans, possesses supernatural perceptual abilities. Such beliefs appear to be influenced and maintained by parental and cultural socialization processes that reinforce such views. Otherwise, little is known about the development of many other facets of children's RS lives, such as how children, while being reared as polytheists, nontheists, atheists, or agnostics, contend with living in cultural contexts dominated by theistic cognitive schemas or how children being reared as theists adapt during childhood to secular contexts that emphasize scientific rather than religious thinking (Cui, Clegg, Yan, Davoodi, Harris, & Corriveau, 2020).

Taking a step back for perspective, some researchers contend that a "healthy" theistic RS orientation involves harmonious congruence among believers' adaptive doctrinal representations of God, experiential representations of God as an attachment figure, and observable behavioral (or procedural) expressions of those doctrinal and experiential representations, just as engaging in public rituals or prayer. For children reared within theistic religious groups, all three aspects – "head" (doctrinal representations), "heart" (experiential representations), and "hands" (behavioral expressions) – presumably need to be well integrated and harmonious to facilitate human well-being as is thought necessary for adults (Davis et al., 2013; Davis et al., 2018). Virtually no studies, however, have addressed children's experiences of the dark side of RS that could unravel such integration. An exception to this rule is Jensen's (2009) descriptive, mixed-methods study that recruited children (ages 7–12), adolescents, and adults from theologically conservative and liberal Presbyterian churches in Washington DC (N = 20 in each of the six groups). Children commonly endorsed a belief in the Devil (89 percent and 50 percent from two types of churches, respectively) and viewed the Devil as possessing supernatural powers, although less so than adolescents and adults. Clearly, more studies are needed to understand the development of children's thoughts or feelings about demonic supernatural entities and the potentially negative impact of these beliefs on children's well-being. Similarly, studies are needed that address at what age and what factors may trigger children to experience doubts or struggles in a felt relationship with God or conflicts with family members about RS issues. That is, more research is needed to clarify when and why some children come to question the truth-value of affirmative God concepts and connections and whether RS experiences would disappear or simply be relegated to the fantasy realm without ongoing familial input and cultural support.

Conclusions: Challenges to Advancing Science on Children's RS

The United Nations (UN) has been discussing children's RS development for nearly a century. The UN's 1989 Convention on the Rights of the Child states that children have the right "to freedom of thought, conscience and religion" and that parents and guardians have the rights and duties "to provide direction to the child in the exercise of his or her right in a manner consistent with the evolving capacities of the child" (Roehlkepartain, 2014; Sagberg, 2017). Ideally, social scientists would offer replicated scientific facts to facilitate international dialogues on ways that children's RS development shapes their psychosocial development, for better or worse. Furthermore, on a planet where approximately 84 percent of humans are affiliated with a religious tradition (Pew Research Center, 2012), it would seem wise to have scientifically based findings to help inform international policy about factors that facilitate or inhibit children from embracing or rejecting RS as they move through early to late childhood and the benefits or costs of differing developmental trajectories centered on RS constructs. Pertinent to such dialogues, this Element offers a whirlwind tour of the emerging social scientific landscape where initial explorations have been conducted into children's RS development. One central observation is that this literature is in its infancy stage. This Element required weaving together disparate bodies of initial investigations conducted by scholars from different disciplinary backgrounds that encompass the fields of religious education, the psychology of RS, the sociology of RS, and cognitive-developmental science. Available studies reveal intriguing initial findings and formidable challenges that social scientists face to advance a balanced and in-depth understanding of children's RS development. This final section revisits key findings and considers ways that scientific inquiry into children's RS could be broadened and deepened in upcoming decades.

Descriptive longitudinal, child-centered RS data. With the remarkable exception of Tamminen's (1994) study using data gathered from Finnish children more than forty years ago, virtually no longitudinal studies exist that track children's RS cognitions and behaviors over time. Furthermore, available cross-sectional research rests largely on relatively small convenience samples or national US surveys of predominantly Christian children drawn from Western societies. Happily, available studies clearly demonstrate that children can very reliably provide self-reported quantitative data on their RS beliefs and behaviors starting as young as age six or seven. Fisher's (1998; 2004; 2011; 2015) studies, for example, offer ample psychometric data on the high reliability of children's reports of a felt relationship with God. Cognitive-developmental scientists have likewise shown that children age of six or older can reliably report on their understanding of both super-natural entities and prayer (e.g., Lane et al., 2010; 2016). In addition, ethno-graphic and qualitative approaches offer valuable insights into children's RS experiences (Mata-McMahon, 2016). Moving forward, it is imperative that longitudinal mixed-method data be collected from children and their parents from diverse RS backgrounds. Such data could capture changes in children's RS from early childhood up to adolescence after which youth have somewhat more freedom to internalize or reject their family and/or community's RS worldviews or practices.

Transparency about transcendence. As the first major section of this Element vividly illustrates, wide variation exists in social scientists' wholistic concep-tual models of children's spiritual development and, puzzlingly, the term "chil-dren's religious development" is virtually absent from this literature. Even more perplexing is the peculiar avoidance of the word "God" in theorizing about children's spiritual well-being. This avoidance belies the fact that available studies involve children whose families are overwhelmingly affiliated with theistic (i.e., deity focused) RS traditions and, with the exception of Stoyles et al. (2012), the assessment tools developed to assess children's spirituality well-being employ the term "God." As is the case in adolescent and adult literatures, social scientists seem more comfortable using euphemisms to refer to children's perceptions of deities in theoretical models of children's RS functioning. These synonyms include, for example, "God, Higher Power, or Ultimate Reality" (Moore et al., 2012), "the transcendent other" (Fisher, 2004), "the divine or ultimate reality" (Sifers et al., 2012), and "divine presence" (Miller, 2015). The adolescent and adult literatures on RS use similar terms (Exline, 2013; King, Ramos, & Clardy, 2013) plus other synonyms, including "the superhuman" in sociology (Smith, 2017) and "the sacred" in psychology (Hill & Pargament, 2008) to refer to self-transcendence as a prototypical feature of spirituality. Yet, considerable ambiguity exists across child and adult literatures as to what objects or "higher powers," if any, individuals are connecting to beyond the self. In an effort to be ecumenical and inclusive, some researchers offer expansive lists of possible foci of self-transcendent connection. For example, Miller (2015, p. 52) articulates that:

> The name or identity of the higher power may differ in the way it is understood across people and traditions, but regardless of those variations, the transcendent relationship opens us into a sense of a sacred world with direction and connection that gives us meaning and purpose. The transcendent relationship may be perceived as a personal dialogue with God, or a sense of oneness with the universe (as it often is in Eastern traditions), or a sense of relationship with a universal spirit through the many living beings and natural forms around us, from majestic mountains to soaring eagles.

Even more explicitly, some social scientists posit that children's RS development does not require human perceptions of supernatural phenomena or relationships, although many people across the globe include deities or other supernatural agents (e.g., deceased immortal ancestors) as central to their RS narratives (Roehlkepartain, 2014).

In dancing around the word "God," social scientists essentially appear to be wrestling with a fundamental tension within the modern world whereby secular worldviews have arisen that understand the universe without reference to any supernatural forces (Nelson, 2009; Thiessen & Wilkins-Laflamme, 2020). Western societies are especially witnessing the rising popularity of nontheistic definitions of spirituality that emphasize a dissolution of duality and the striving for a transpersonal sense of oneness with the natural world without endorsing supernatural phenomena (Santos & Michaels, 2020). Wholistic models of children's RS development appear to reflect efforts to generate a universal model that reconciles theistic (i.e., God-centered) and nontheistic models of RS. Yet, as seen in Table 1, in efforts to be maximally inclusive when theorizing about children's RS development, social scientists risk obscuring the fact that God is, thus far, the consistently unique element that differentiates wholistic measures of children's RS from children's self-esteem and social relationships (e.g., family, peers, other adults) in scientific studies.

Moving forward, researchers need to be transparent about what makes their conceptualization and assessment tools to investigate children's RS development distinctive from other models of children's development, particularly the roles of their relationships with other people and the self. Furthermore, researchers need to use construct labels that do not obscure the items used in measures. For example, a study by Kendler, Gardner, and Prescott (1997) has been framed as capturing a beneficial dimension of "children's spirituality" (e.g., Miller, 2015). However, the relevant subscale that Kendler et al. (1997) created encompassed both public and private forms of RS. Specifically, in this study the five items were importance of religion, frequency of church attendance, consciousness of religious purpose, seeking spiritual comfort, and private prayer. Notably, Kendler et al. (1997) clearly referred to this scale as an index of religious "personal devotion." In addition, progress on children's RS will be enhanced by researchers being transparent about (1) how subscales that assess children's RS development do and do not overlap with children's involvement in organized religious groups and (2) children's exposure to ideas about supernatural agents widely promoted within their broader cultural context, even if some children or their families do not endorse such beliefs.

RS for better and worse. Another way to advance literature on children's RS development is for researchers to generate scientific evidence that differentiates adaptive and maladaptive RS processes that children employ in their daily lives as well as during times of trouble. This topic emerged as an urgent area for further investigation in the second section of this Element. Studies based on global indicators of child or parental RS paint a far from rosy picture of the roles of RS within children's lives, including mixed findings from preliminary studies that have employed children as participants. These inconsistent findings preclude easy generalizations about higher parental or child RS being tied to better child psychosocial adjustment. Moving forward, disentangling less common but potent RS struggles from more commonplace RS resources is likely to produce more clear and robust results.

To elaborate, most studies to date employ content-free mechanisms of engaging in RS activities, such as how frequently a child or parent attends religious services or engages in private prayer. Such indices reveal little about those RS activities that could be helpful or harmful because such indices do not capture the substance of RS thoughts and feelings (e.g., feeling loved by versus cut off from God) or RS behaviors with others (e.g., supportive or conflictual dialogues about faith) that could enhance or undermine children's psychosocial adjustment. A lack of specificity in global RS indices leaves ample room for researchers to speculate that higher parental RS (e.g., religious attendance) increases the risk that children will be subjected to corporal punishment and/ or child physical abuse due to parents' internalizing specific religious scriptures or theological teachings that encourage harmful parental behavior. Notably, although parents who endorse or are affiliated with conservative Christian groups are more likely to use corporal punishment with young children, the opposite conclusion generally applies to higher religious attendance at any place of worship – that is, most studies find that parents' higher religious attendance is tied to lower parental physical aggression. Conversely, when nonspecific measures of RS yield salutary findings, social scientists can easily attribute potential benefits of RS to generic psychosocial processes, such as social support, rather than anything unique about RS, such as gaining a sense of comfort, love, or empowerment from a deity or RS community. Studies are needed that delve into specific RS constructs (e.g., positive and negative RS coping, sanctification) that do not have obvious secular parallels. Such research could provide parents and professionals who work with children with valuable insights about ways faith can function as a unique resource or risk to their psychological and social well-being (Mahoney, Pomerleau, & Riley, 2019). Finally, almost no systematic studies exist about children harboring fears about demonic forces or parents utilizing RS in coercive ways to back up their parental authority or justify harsh parenting practices. More in-depth and specific indices are likely to yield more insights into the dark side of RS while simultaneously showing that benefits are most likely for youth who possess well-integrated and high levels of RS and risks least likely for non-RS youth.

Parental and familial socialization of RS cross-culturally. A fourth direction for expansion is to dramatically increase cross-cultural investigations to broaden our understanding of the roles that parents and families play in influencing children's RS development. The third section of this Element highlighted that parents in Western cultures, intentionally or not, powerfully shape their children's RS development. Furthermore, at least within the United States, parents from diverse religious traditions concur that for their children to become good and happy adults, they need to develop a firm sense of self that is rooted in their parents' RS beliefs and values. Most US parents, however, are not concerned about their children learning the particular doctrinal claims or specific teachings of a given religious tradition. Instead, US parents hope their children gain a sense of self-transcendence via belief in benevolent supernatural forces while at the same time avoiding dogmatically imposing their RS views on others. According to Smith and Admaczyk's (2021) synthesis, such parental attitudes accommodate and reflect a broader US cultural model of parenthood that strongly encourages parents to facilitate their children's sense of individuality and autonomy in directing their lives. Furthermore, only around one-third of US parents report that their top parenting goal is to rear children "whose lives reflect God's will and purpose" whereas around another one-third rank this goal as dead last. Such findings hint at the growing polarization within the United States, and potentially across the globe, about the core agendas that parents from diverse RS backgrounds in different cultural contexts may have for childbearing and rearing. Clearly, more cross-cultural scientific research is imperative to better understand the fundamental similarities and differences in parents' attitudes and behaviors about optimal methods to rear children based on parents' convictions about the positive or negative roles that RS can play in peoples' lives.

Avoiding reductionism. The fourth section of this Element delineated the efforts of cognitive-developmental scientists to uncover universal cognitive processes that underlie children's understandings of supernatural agents. Once again, virtually all of these studies focus on children's concepts of God, and the findings document that children can and do reliably differentiate God's supernatural abilities from humans' abilities around age five or six. Likewise, around this age, children appear to grasp the nature of prayer to God and can reliably report on their experiences of this practice. Barrett (2012) and others' interpretations of initial findings about young children's attributions of God's omniscience have contributed to controversial debates about whether humans have evolved to be "naturally prepared" to comprehend and distinguish theistic deities from human/parental agents. Research suggests that the key issues are whether children's broader cultural content as well as specific RS socialization by families supports and reinforces children's understandings of supernatural agents over time, however irrational such perceptions may seem to some people. Far more studies are needed with larger family samples drawn from diverse geographical regions of the globe and with children reared in varying secular and RS communities. Many of children's RS cognitions likely mirror their thinking about magical or fantasy characters more generally. Nevertheless, a *central* point for social scientists to consider is that the psychosocial implications over time of children's RS cognitions may yield qualitatively different outcomes *precisely because* children's families and broader social contexts sustain the ongoing persistence of substantively unique beliefs and behaviors tied to supernatural phenomena over the lifespan. Rather than merely reduce RS believing, bonding, behaving, and belonging to what social scientists may assume are more fundamental human processes, societies need scientifically based insights into the power of RS itself, for better and worse, across diverse cultures (Pargament et al., 2013; Saroglou, 2011).

Religious traditions and children's RS development . Finally, social scientists who venture into challenging research on children's RS development should consider the degree to which organized religious traditions continue to function as the primary cultural institutions that speak to the RS dimension of children's development. Research that extracts the concept of children's spiritual development out of broader religious and cultural contexts likely forces hard but untenable conceptual boundaries between children's "self" RS development and ways their family, peer, and school-based relationships are shaped by organized religious groups. Although participation in organized religious groups has declined over recent decades in the United States, Canada, Europe, and Australia, child-focused researchers may want to keep in mind that conceptualizing R and S as being mutually exclusive domains probably tends to be most relevant to a relatively narrow slice of the global demographic pie: children from more educated and affluent families located within individualistically oriented Western societies. Otherwise, for better or worse, religious institutions continue to represent a major conduit by which many children, parents, and teachers across the globe are exposed to messages about the nature and role that perceived supernatural phenomena could play for children's development. To advance research on children's RS, it behooves researchers to delve into the details about the overlapping domains of R and S. In the process, social scientists need to be as explicit as possible about what particular aspects of RS their conceptual models, methods, and research questions address for the children and families who are participating in a given study.

Closing comments. This Element has offered a comprehensive yet concise account of what scientists do and do not know about children's RS development to spur further scientific investigation into unique benefits and risks that RS can play in children's lives. Conspicuously absent from this Element are comprehensive theoretical models that integrate contemporary mainstream science about *children's* biological, psychological, social, educational, and moral developmental processes across diverse cultures with the up-to-date empirical findings on children's RS. Why this silence? Because such integrative developmental models still need to be created that target childhood. Such theoretical work will be important because children's experiences with RS likely set the stage for adolescents and adults being able to achieve a well-integrated (non)RS identity that provides them with firmly moored yet flexible responses to existential dilemmas that everyone faces across the lifespan. Hopefully this Element will help to inspire much needed theoretical and empirical work to help the budding science of children's RS development rapidly blossom in the coming decades.

References

Abar, B., Carter, K. L., & Winsler, A. (2009). The effects of maternal parenting style and religious commitment on self-regulation, academic achievement, and risk behavior among African-American parochial college students. *Journal of Adolescence, 32*(2), 259–73. https://doi.org/10.1016/j.adolescence.2008.03.008

Abbotts, J. E., Williams, R. G. A., Sweeting, H. N., & West, P. B. (2004). Is going to church good or bad for you? Denomination, attendance and mental health of children in West Scotland. *Social Science and Medicine, 58*, 645–56. https://doi.org/10.1016/S0277-9536(03)00283-1

Abu-Raiya, H., & Pargament, K. I. (2015). Religious coping among diverse religions: Commonalities and divergences. *Psychology of Religion and Spirituality, 7*(1), 24–33. https://doi.org/10.1037/a0037652

Avinun, R., Davidov, M., Mankuta, D., & Knafo-Noam, A. (2018). Predicting the use of corporal punishment: Child aggression, parent religiosity, and the BDNF gene. *Aggressive Behavior, 44*(2), 165–75. https://doi.org/10.1002/ab.21740

Bader, C., & Desmond, S. (2006). Do as I say and as I do: The effects of consistent parental beliefs and behaviors upon religious transmission, *Sociology of Religion 67*(3), 313–29.

Bamford, C., & Lagattuta, K. H. (2010). A new look at children's understanding of mind and emotion: The case of prayer. *Developmental Psychology, 46*(1), 78–92. https://doi.org/10.1037/a0016694

Barrett, J. L. (2012). *Born Believers: The Science of Childhood Religion.* New York: The Free Press.

Barrett, J. L., Newman, R., & Richert, R. A. (2003). When seeing does not lead to believing: Children's understanding of the importance of background knowledge for interpreting visual displays. *Journal of Cognition & Culture, 3*(1), 91–108. https://doi.org/10.1163/156853703321598590

Barrett, J. L., & Richert, R. A. (2003). Anthropomorphism or preparedness? Exploring children's God concepts. *Review of Religious Research 44*(3), 300–12. www.jstor.org/stable/3512389

Barrett, J. L., Richert, R. A., & Driesenga, A. (2001). God's beliefs versus mother's: The development of nonhuman agent concepts. *Child Development, 72*(1), 50–65. https://doi.org/10.1111/1467-8624.00265

Barrow, B. H., Dollahite, D. C., & Marks, L. D. (2020, January 13). How parents balance desire for religious continuity with honoring children's religious agency. *Psychology of Religion and Spirituality.* Advance online publication. http://dx.doi.org/10.1037/rel0000307

Barry, C. M., Christofferson, J. L., Boorman, E., & Nelson, L. J. (2020). Profiles of religiousness, spirituality, and psychological adjustment in emerging adults. *Journal of Adult Development, 27*, 201–11. https://doi .org/10.1007/s10804-019-09334-z

Bartkowski, J. P., Xu, X., & Bartkowski, S. (2019). Mixed blessing: The beneficial and detrimental effects of religion on child development among third-graders. *Religions, 10*, 37. https://doi.org/10.3390/rel10010037

Bartkowski, J. P., Xu, X., & Levin, M. L. (2008). Religion and child development: Evidence from the early childhood longitudinal study. *Social Science Research, 37*(1), 18–36. https://doi.org/10.1016/j.ssrese arch.2007.02.001

Bengtson, V. L., Copen, C. E., Putney, N. M., & Silverstein, M. (2009). A longitudinal study of the intergenerational transmission of religion. *International Sociology, 24*(3), 325–45. https://doi.org/10.1177/0268580909 102911

Bengtson, V. L., Hayward, R. D., Zuckerman, P., & Silverstein, M. (2018). Bringing up the nones: Intergenerational influences and cohort trends. *Journal for the Scientific Study of Religion, 57*(2), 258–75. http://dx.doi.org /10.1111/jssr.12511

Bengtson, V. L., Putney, N., & Harris, S. C. (2013). *Families and Faith: How Religion Is Passed Down across Generations*. New York. NY: Oxford University Press.

Benore, E., Pargament, K. I., & Pendleton, S. (2008). An initial examination of religious coping in children with asthma. *International Journal for the Psychology of Religion, 18*(4), 267–90. https://doi.org /10.1080/10508610802229197

Bornstein, M. H., Putnick, D. L., Lansford, J. E., Al-Hassan, S. M., Bacchini, D., Bombi, A. S., Chang, L., Deater-Deckard, K., Di Giunta, L., Dodge, K. A., Malone, P. S., Oburu, P., Pastorelli, C., Skinner, A. T., Sorbring, E., Steinberg, L., Tapanya, S., Tirado, L., Zelli, A., & Alampay, L. P. (2017). "Mixed blessings": Parental religiousness, parenting, and child adjustment in global perspective. *Journal of Child Psychology and Psychiatry, and Allied Disciplines, 58*(8), 880–92. https://doi.org/10.1111 /jcpp.12705

Boyatzis, C. J. (ed.) (2003). Religious and spiritual development: An introduction. *Review of Religious Research, 44*(3), 213–19.

Boyatzis, C. J. (2006). Unraveling the dynamics of religion in the family and parent-child relationships. *The International Journal for the Psychology of Religion, 16*(4), 245–51.

Boyatzis, C. J. (2012). Spiritual development during childhood and adolescence. In L. Miller (ed.), *The Oxford Handbook of Psychology and Spirituality* (pp. 151–64). Oxford University Press.

Boyatzis, C. J. (2013). The nature and functions of religion and spirituality in children. In K. I. Pargament, J. J. Exline, & J. W. Jones (eds.), *APA Handbook of Psychology, Religion, and Spirituality: Context, Theory, and Research* (vol. 1, pp. 497–512). American Psychological Association. https://doi.org /10.1037/14045-027

Boyatzis, C. J., & Janicki, D. (2003). Parent-child communication about religion: A survey and diary assessment of unilateral transmission and bi-directional reciprocity. *Review of Religious Research, 44*(3), 252–70.

Bronfenbrenner, U., & Morris, P. A. (2006). The bioecological model of human development. In R. M. Lerner & W. Damon (eds.), *Handbook of Child Psychology: Theoretical Models of Human Development* (vol. 1, pp. 793–828). Hoboken, NJ: Wiley.

Breyer, R. J., & MacPhee, D. (2015). Community characteristics, conservative ideology, and child abuse rates. *Child Abuse & Neglect, 41*, 126–35. https:// doi.org/10.1016/j.chiabu.2014.11.019

Bryant-Davis, T., Ellis, M. U., Burke-Maynard, E., Moon, N., Counts, P. A., & Anderson, G. (2012). Religiosity, spirituality, and trauma recovery in the lives of children and adolescents. *Professional Psychology: Research and Practice, 43*(4), 306–14. https://doi.org/10.1037/a0029282

Burdett, E. R. R, & Barrett, J. L. (2016). The circle of life: A cross cultural comparison of children's attribution of life cycle traits. *British Journal of Developmental Psychology, 34*(2), 276–90. https://doi.org/10.1111/bjdp .12131

Burdett, E. R. R., Wigger, J. B., & Barrett, J. L. (2019). The minds of God, mortals, and in-betweens: Children's developing understanding of extraordinary and ordinary minds across four countries. *Psychology of Religion and Spirituality.* Advance online publication. https://doi.org/10.1037 /rel0000285

Burdett, E. R. R., Barrett, J. L., & Greenway, T. S. (2020). Children's developing understanding of the cognitive abilities of supernatural and natural minds: Evidence from three cultures. *Journal for the Study of Religion, Nature and Culture, 14*(1), 124–151. https://doi.org/10.1558/jsrnc.39186

Cassiba, R., Granqvist, P., & Costantini, A. (2013). Mothers' attachment security predicts their children's sense of God's closeness. *Attachment & Human Development, 15*(1), 51–64. https://doi.org/10.1080/14616734 .2013.743253

Cavalletti, S. (1992). *The Religious Potential of the Child.* Chicago, IL: Archdioceses of Chicago – Liturgy Training Publications.

Champagne, E. (2003). Being a child, a spiritual child. *International Journal of Children's Spirituality, 8*(1), 43–53.

Cheung, C. K., & Yeung, J. W. K. (2011). Meta-analysis of relationships between religiosity and constructive and destructive behaviors among adolescents. *Children and Youth Services Review, 33*(2), 376–85. https://doi.org/10.1016/j.childyouth.2010.10.004

Coles, R. (1990). *The Spiritual Life of Children.* Boston, MA: Houghton Mifflin.

Cotton, S., McGrady, M., & Rosenthal, S. (2006). Measurement of religiosity/ spirituality in adolescent health outcomes research: Trends and recommendations. *Journal of Religion & Health, 49*(4), 414–44. https://doi.org/10.1016/j.jadohealth.2005.10.005

Cremeens, J., Eiser, C., & Blades, M. (2006). Characteristics of health-related self-report measures for children aged three to eight years: A review of the literature. *Quality of Life Research, 15,* 739–54. https://doi.org/10.1007/s11136-005-4184-x

Crosby, R. G. III, & Smith, E. I. (2017). Measuring children's church-based social support: Development and initial validation of the kids' church survey. *Social Development, 26*(2), 423–42. https://doi.org/10.1111/sode.12198

Cui, Y. K., Clegg, J. M., Yan, E. F., Davoodi, T., Harris, P. L., & Corriveau, K. H. (2020). Religious testimony in a secular society: Belief in unobservable entities among Chinese parents and their children. *Developmental Psychology, 56*(1), 117–27. https://doi.org/10.1037/dev0000846

Davis, K. A., & Epkins, C. C. (2009). Do private religious practices moderate the relation between family conflict and preadolescents' depression and anxiety symptoms? *Journal of Early Adolescence, 29*(5), 693–717. https://doi.org/10.1177/0272431608325503

Davis, E. B., Granqvist, P., & Sharp, C. (2018). Theistic relational spirituality: Development, dynamics, health, and transformation. *Psychology of Religion and Spirituality.* Advance online publication. http://doi.org./10.1037/rel0000219

Davis, E. B., Moriarty, G. L., & Mauch, J. C. (2013). God images and god concepts: Definitions, development, and dynamics. *Psychology of Religion and Spirituality, 5*(1), 51–60. https://doi.org/10.1037/a0029289

De Roos, S. A., Miedema, S., & Iedema, J. (2001). Attachment, working models of self and others, and God concept in kindergarten. *Journal for the Scientific Study of Religion, 40*(4), 607–18. https://doi.org/10.1111/0021-8294.00080

De Smedt, J. & De Cruz, H. (2020). *The Challenge of Evolution to Religion.* Cambridge, UK: Cambridge University Press.

Desrosiers, A., Kelly, B. S., & Miller, L. (2011). Parent and peer relationships and relational spirituality in adolescents and young adults. *Psychology of Religion and Spirituality*, *3*(1), 39–54. https://doi.org/10.1037/a0020037

Dickie, J. R., Eshleman, A. K., Merasco, D. M., Shepard, A., VanderWilt, M., & Johnson, M. (1997). Parent-child relationships and children's images of God. *Journal for the Scientific Study of Religion*, *36*(1), 25–43. https://doi.org/10.2307/1387880

Dollahite, D., Marks, L., Babcock, K., Barrow, B., & Rose, A. (2019). Beyond religious rigidities: Religious firmness and religious flexibility as complementary loyalties in faith transmission. *Religions*, *10*(2), 111. http://dx.doi.org/10.3390/rel10020111

Dumas, J. E., & Nissley-Tsiopinis, J. (2006). Parental global religiousness, sanctification of parenting, and positive and negative religious coping as predictors of parental and child functioning. *International Journal for the Psychology of Religion*, *16*(4), 289–310. https://doi.org/10.1207/s15327582ijpr1604_4

Dyslin, C., & Thomsen, C. (2005). Religiosity and risk of perpetrating child physical abuse: An empirical investigation. *Journal of Psychology and Theology*, *33*(4), 291–98. https://doi.org/10.1177/009164710503300405

Ellison, C. G., & Bradshaw, M. (2009). Religious beliefs, sociopolitical ideology, and attitudes toward corporal punishment. *Journal of Family Issues*, *30*(3), 320–40. https://doi.org/10.1177/0192513X08326331

Ellison, C. G., Bartkowski, J. P., & Segal, M. L. (1996). Do conservative Protestant parents spank more often? Further evidence from the national survey of families and households. *Social Science Quarterly*, *77*(3), 663–73.

Ellison, C. G., & McFarland, M. J. (2013). The social context of religion and spirituality in the United States. In K. I. Pargament, J. J. Exline, & J. W. Jones (eds.), *APA Handbook of Psychology, Religion, and Spirituality: Context, Theory, and Research* (vol. 1, pp. 21–50). American Psychological Association. https://doi.org/10.1037/14045-002

Ellison, C. G., Musick, M. A., & Holden, G. W. (2011). Does conservative Protestantism moderate the association between corporal punishment and child outcomes? *Journal of Marriage and Family*, *73*(5), 946–61. https://doi.org/10.1111/j.1741-3737.2011.00854.x

Exline, J. J. (2013). Religious and spiritual struggles. In K. I. Pargament, J. J. Exline, & J. W. Jones (eds.), *APA Handbook of Psychology, Religion, and Spirituality: Context, Theory, and Research* (vol. 1, pp. 459–76). American Psychological Association. https://doi.org/10.1037/14045-025

Exline, J. J., Pargament, K. I., Grubbs, J. B., & Yali, A. M. (2014). The Religious and Spiritual Struggles Scale: Development and initial validation. *Psychology of Religion and Spirituality*, *6*(3), 208–22. https://doi.org/10.1037/a0036465

Exline, J. J., Yali, A. M., & Sanderson, W. C. (2000). Guilt, discord, and alienation: The role of religious strain in depression and suicidality. *Journal of Clinical Psychology*, *56*(12), 1481–96. http://dx.doi.org/10.1002/1097-4679(200012)56:12 1481::AID-13.0.CO;2-A

Fisher, J. W. (1998). Spiritual health: Its nature, and place in the school curriculum. Doctoral dissertation. The University of Melbourne, Melbourne, Victoria, Australia.

Fisher, J. W. (2004). Feeling good, living life: A spiritual health measure for young children. *Journal of Beliefs & Values*, *25*(3), 307–15. https://doi.org/10.1080/1361767042000306121

Fisher, J. W. (2009). Getting the balance: Assessing spirituality and well-being among children and youth. *International Journal of Children's Spirituality*, *14*(3), 273–88. https://doi.org/10.1080/13644360903086547

Fisher, J. W. (2011). The four domains model: Connecting spirituality, health and well-being. *Religions*, *2*, 17–28. https://doi.org/10.3390/rel2010017

Fisher, J. W. (2015). God counts for children's spiritual well-being. *International Journal of Children's Spirituality*, *20*(3–4), 191–203. https://doi.org/10.1080/1364436X.2015.1107033

Fisher, J. W., Francis, L. J., & Johnson, P. (2000) Assessing spiritual health via four domains of well-being: The SH4DI. *Pastoral Psychology*, *49*(2), 133–45. https://doi.org/10.1023/A:1004609227002

Fowler, J. W. (1981). *Stages of Faith: The Psychology of Human Development and the Quest for Meaning*. New York: HarperCollins.

Fowler, J. W. (1996). *Faithful Change: The Personal and Public Challenges of Postmodern Life*. Nashville, TN: Abingdon Press.

Frechette, S., & Romano, E. (2015). Change in corporal punishment over time in a representative sample of Canadian parents. *Journal of Family Psychology*, *29*(4), 507–17. https://doi.org/10.1037/fam0000104

French, D. C., Eisenberg, N., Sallquist, J., Purwono, U., Lu, T., & Christ, S. (2013). Parent-adolescent relationships, religiosity, and the social adjustment of Indonesian Muslim adolescents. *Journal of Family Psychology*, *27*(3), 421–30. https://doi.org/10.1037/a0032858

Gallagher, S., Phillips, A. C., Lee, H., & Carroll, D. (2015). The association between spirituality and depression in parents caring for children with developmental disabilities: Social support and/or last resort. *Journal of Religion and Health*, *54*(1), 358–70. https://doi.org/10.1007/s10943-014-9839-x

Gershoff, E. T., Goodman, G. S., Miller-Perrin, C. L., Holden, G. W., Jackson, Y., & Kazdin, A. E. (2018). The strength of the causal evidence against physical punishment of children and its implications for parents, psychologists, and policymakers. *American Psychologist, 73*(5), 626–38. https://doi.org/10.1037/amp0000327

Giménez-Dasí, M., Guerrero, S., & Harris, P. L. (2005). Intimations of immortality and omniscience in early childhood. *European Journal of Developmental Psychology, 2*(3), 285–97. https://doi.org/10.1080 /17405620544000039

Gomez, R., & Fisher, J. W. (2003) Domains of spiritual well-being and development and validation of the Spiritual Well-Being Questionnaire. *Personality and Individual Differences, 35*(8), 1975–91. https://doi.org/10 .1016/S0191-8869(03)00045-X

Granqvist, P. (2020). *Attachment in Religion and Spirituality: A Wider View.* New York: Guilford Press.

Granqvist, P., & Kirkpatrick, L. A. (2013). Religion, spirituality, and attachment. In K. I. Pargament, J. J. Exline, & J. W. Jones (eds.), *APA Handbook of Psychology, Religion, and Spirituality: Context, Theory, and Research* (vol. 1, pp. 139–56). Washington, DC: American Psychological Association. https://doi.org/10.1037/14045-007

Granqvist, P., Ljungdahl, C., & Dickie, J. (2007). God is nowhere, God is now here: Attachment activation, security of attachment, and God's perceived closeness among 5–7-year-old children from religious and nonreligious homes. *Attachment & Human Development, 9*(1), 55–71. https://doi.org/10 .1080/14616730601151458

Grogan-Kaylora, A., Burlakab, V., Mac, J., Leea, S., Castilloa, B., and Churakovab, I. (2018). Predictors of parental use of corporal punishment in Ukraine. *Children and Youth Services Review, 88*, 66–73. https://doi.org/10 .1016/j.childyouth.2018.03.003

Gurrentz, B. T. (2017). Family formation and close social ties within religious congregations. *Journal of Marriage and Family, 79*(4), 1125–43. https://doi .org/10.1111/jomf.12398

Hammer, J. H., Wade, N. G., & Cragun, R. T. (2020). Valid assessment of spiritual quality of life with the WHOQOL-SRPB BREF across religious, spiritual, and secular persons: A psychometric study. *Psychology of Religion and Spirituality, 12*(4), 440–50. https://doi.org/10.1037/rel0000266

Hardy, S. A., Dollahite, D. C., & Baldwin, C. R. (2019, online). Parenting, religion, and moral development. In D. J. Laible, G. Carlo, & L. M. Padilla-Walker (eds.), *The Oxford Handbook of Parenting and Moral Development.* New York: Oxford University Press. https://doi:10.1093/oxfordhb/ 9780190638696.013.18

Hardy, S. A., Nelson, J. M., Moore, J. P., & King, P. E. (2019). Processes of religious and spiritual influence in adolescence: A systematic review of 30 years of research. *Journal of Research on Adolescence, 29*(2), 254–75. https://onlinelibrary.wiley.com/doi/abs/10.1111/jora.12486

Hardy, S. A., White, J. A., Zhang, Z., & Ruchty, J. (2011). Parenting and the socialization of religiousness and spirituality. *Psychology of Religion and Spirituality, 3*(3), 217–30. https://doi.org/10.1037/a0021600

Hay, D., & Nye, R. (1998). *The Spirit of the Child*. London and Philadelphia: Jessica Kingsley Publishers.

Hill, P. C., & Edwards, E. (2013). Measurement in the psychology of religiousness and spirituality. In K. I. Pargament, J. J. Exline, & J. W. Jones (eds.), *APA Handbook of Psychology, Religion, and Spirituality: Context, Theory, and Research* (vol. 1, pp. 51–78). Washington, DC: American Psychological Association. https://doi.org/10.1037/14045-003

Hill, P. C., & Pargament, K. I. (2008). Advances in the conceptualization and measurement of religion and spirituality: Implications for physical and mental health research. *Psychology of Religion and Spirituality*, S(1), 3–17. https://doi.org/10.1037/1941-1022.S.1.3

Hoffmann, J., Ellison, C., & Bartkowski, J. (2017). Conservative Protestantism and attitudes toward corporal punishment, 1986–2014. *Social Science Research, 63*, 81–94. https://doi.org/10.1016/j.ssresearch.2016.09.010

Holder, M. D., Coleman,B., & J. M. Wallace. (2010). Spirituality, religiousness, and happiness in children aged 8–12 years. *Journal of Happiness Studies, 11*(2), 131–50. https://doi.org/10.1007/s10902-008-9126-1

Holden, G. W., & Vittrup, B. (2010). Religion. In M. H. Bornstein (ed.), *Handbook of Cultural Developmental Science* (pp. 279–95). New York: Psychology Press.

Holden G. W., & Williamson P.A. (2014). Religion and child well-being. In A. Ben-Arieh, F. Casas, I. Frønes, & J. Korbin (eds.), *Handbook of Child Well-Being* (pp. 1137–69). New York: Springer. https://doi.org/10.1007/978-90-481-9063-8_158

Holder, M. D., Coleman, B., Krupa, T., & Krupa, E. (2016). Well-being's relation to religiosity and spirituality in children and adolescents in Zambia. *Journal of Happiness Studies* 17, 1235–53. https://doi.org/10.1007/s10902-015-9640-x

Hood, R. W, Hill, P. C., & Spilka, B. (2018). *Psychology of Religion: An Empirical Approach* (5th ed.). New York: Guilford Press.

Howell, K. H., Shapiro, D. N., Layne, C. M., & Kaplow, J. G. (2015) Individual and psychosocial mechanisms of adaptive functioning in parentally bereaved children. *Death Studies*, *39*(5), 296–306. https://doi.org/10.1080/07481187.2014.951497

Idler, E. L., Musick, M. A., Ellison, C. G., George, L. K., Krause, N., Ory, M. G., Pargament, K. I., Powell, L. H., Underwood, L. G., & Williams, D. R. (2003). Measuring multiple dimensions of religion and spirituality for health research. *Research on Aging*, *25*(4), 327–65. https://journals.sagepub.com/doi/10.1177/0164027503025004001

Jensen, L. A. (2009). Conceptions of God and the Devil across the lifespan: A cultural- developmental study of religious liberals and conservatives. *Journal for the Scientific Study of Religion*, *48*(1), 121–45. https://doi.org/10.1111/j.1468-5906.2009.01433.x

Jirojanakul, P., & Skevington, S. (2000). Developing a quality of life measure for children aged 5–8 years. *British Journal of Health Psychology*, *5*(3), 299–321. https://doi.org/10.1348/135910700168937

Kapuscinski, A. N., & Masters, K. S. (2010). The current status of measures of spirituality: A critical review of scale development. *Psychology of Religion and Spirituality*, *2*(4), 191–205. https://doi.org/10.1037/a0020498

Kelley, H. H., Galbraith, Q., & Korth, B. B. (2020). The how and what of modern religious transmission and its implications for families. *Journal of Family Psychology*. Advance online publication. https://doi.org/10.1037/fam0000673

Kendler, K. S., Gardner, C. O., & Prescott, C. A. (1997). Religion, psychopathology, and substance use and abuse: A multimeasure, genetic-epidemiologic study. *American Journal of Psychiatry*, *154*(3), 322–29. https://doi.org/0.1176/ajp.154.3.322

Kiessling, F., & Perner, J. (2014). God–mother–baby: What children think they know. *Child Development*, *85*(4), 1601–16. https://doi.org/10.1111/cdev.12210

Kim, J., McCullough, M., & Chicchetti, D. (2009). Parents' and children's religiosity and child behavioral adjustment among maltreated and nonmaltreated children. *Journal of Child and Family Studies*, *18*(6), 594–605. https://doi.org/:10.1007/s10826-009-9262-1

King, P. E., & Boyatzis, C. J. (2015). Religious and spiritual development. In M. E. Lamb (ed.), *Socioemotional Processes: Handbook of Child Psychology and Developmental Science* (7th ed., vol. 3, pp. 975–1021). Hoboken, NJ: Wiley.

King, P. E., Furrow, J. L., & Roth, N. (2002). The influence of families and peers on adolescent religiousness. *Journal of Psychology and Christianity*, *21*(2), 109–20.

King, P. E., Ramos, J. S., & Clardy, C. E. (2013). Searching for the sacred: Religion, spirituality, and adolescent development. In K. I. Pargament,

J. J. Exline, & J. W. Jones (eds.), *APA Handbook of Psychology, Religion, and Spirituality: Context, Theory, and Research* (vol. 1, pp. 513–28). Washington, DC: American Psychological Association. https://doi.org/10.1037/14045-028

Knight, N., Sousa, P., Barrett, J. L., & Atran, S. (2004). Children's attributions of beliefs to humans and God: Cross-cultural evidence. *Cognitive Science, 28* (1), 117–26. https://doi.org/10.1016/j.cogsci.2003.09.002

Koenig, H. G., McCullough, M. E., & Larson, D. B. (2001). *Handbook of Religion and Health*. New York: Oxford University Press.

Lam, V. L., & Guerrero, S. (2020). Animals, superman, fairy and god: Children's attributions of nonhuman agent beliefs in Madrid and London. *Journal of Cognition and Culture, 20*(1–2), 66–87. https://doi.org/10.1163 /15685373-12340074

Landor, A., Simons, L. G., Simons, R. L., Brody, G. H., & Gibbons, F. X. (2011). The role of religiosity in the relationship between parents, peers, and adolescent risky sexual behavior. *Journal of Youth and Adolescence, 40*(3), 296–309. https://doi.org/10.1007/s10964-010-9598-2

Lane, J. D. (2020). Probabilistic reasoning in context: Socio-cultural differences in children's and adults' predictions about the fulfillment of prayers and wishes. *Journal of Cognition and Development, 21*(2), 240–60. https://doi .org/10.1080/15248372.2019.1709468

Lane, J. D., Evans, E. M., Brink, K. A., & Wellman, H. M. (2016). Developing concepts of ordinary and extraordinary communication. *Developmental Psychology, 52*(1), 19–30. https://doi.org/10.1037/dev0000061

Lane, J. D., Wellman, H. W., & Evans, E. M. (2010). Children's understanding of ordinary and extraordinary minds. *Child Development, 81*(5), 1475–89. https://srcd.onlinelibrary.wiley.com/doi/10.1111/j.1467-8624.2010.01486.x

Lane, J. D., Wellman, H. M., & Evans, E. M. (2012). Socio-cultural input facilitates children's developing understanding of extraordinary minds. *Child Development, 83*(3), 1007–21. https://www.ncbi.nlm.nih.gov/pmc/art icles/PMC3342412

Legare, C. H., Evans, E. M., Rosengren, K. S., & Harris, P. L. (2012). The coexistence of natural and supernatural explanations across cultures and development. *Child Development, 83*(3), 779–93. https://doi.org/10.1111/j .1467-8624.2012.01743.x

Li, S. D. (2013). Familial religiosity, family processes, and juvenile delinquency in a national sample of early adolescents. *The Journal of Early Adolescence, 34*(4), 436–62. https://doi.org/10.1177/0272431613495445

Long, D., Elkind, D., & Spilka, B. (1967). The child's conception of prayer. *Journal for the Scientific Study of Religion, 6*(1), 101–09. https://doi.org/10 .2307/1384202

Longo, G. S., Bray, B. C., & Kim-Spoon, J. (2017). Profiles of adolescent religiousness using latent profile analysis: Implications for psychopathology. *British Journal of Developmental Psychology*, *35*(1), 91–105. https://doi.org/10.1111/bjdp.12183

Mahoney, A. (2010). Religion in families 1999–2009: A relational spirituality framework. *Journal of Marriage and Family*, *72*(4), 805–27. https://doi.org /10.1111/j.1741-3737.2010.00732.x

Mahoney, A., & Boyatzis, C. J. (2019). Parenting, religion, and spirituality. In M. Bornstein (ed.), *Handbook of Parenting* (3rd ed.), pp. 516–52. New York and London: Routledge.

Mahoney, A., Larrid, I. E., Payne, K. K., & Manning, W. D. (2015). Religiosity and US single, cohabiting and married mothers (FP-15-06). National Center for Family & Marriage Research, Bowling Green State University. www.bgsu.edu/resourcesldata/family-profilelsmahoney-lamidi-payne-fp-15-06.html

Mahoney, A., Pargament, K. I., Swank, A., & Tarakeshwar, N. (2001). Religion in the home in the 1980s and '90s: A meta-analytic review and conceptual analysis of religion, marriage, and parenting. *Journal of Family Psychology*, *15*(4), 559–96. https://doi.org/10.1037//0893-3200.15.4.559

Mahoney, A. (2013). The spirituality of us: Relational spirituality in the context of family relationships. In K. Pargament, J. J. Exline, J. Jones, A. Mahoney, & E. Shafranske (eds.), *APA Handbook of Psychology, Religion, and Spirituality* (vol. 2, pp. 365–89). Washington, DC: American Psychological Association. https://doi.org/10.1037/14045-020

Mahoney, A., Pomerleau, J. M., & Riley, A. (2019). Transcending barriers to build bridges between family psychology and religious organizations. In B. H. Fiese, M. Celano, K. Deater-Deckard, E. N. Jouriles, & M. A. Whisman (eds.), *APA Handbook of Contemporary Family Psychology* (vol. 2, pp. 315–35). Washington, DC: APA Publications.

Mahoney, A., Pendleton, S., & Ihrke, H. (2006). Religious coping by children and adolescents: Unexplored territory in the realm of spiritual development. In E. C. Roehlkepartain, P. Ebstyneking, M. Wagener, & P. L. Benson (eds.), *The Handbook of Spiritual Development in Childhood and Adolescence* (pp. 341–54). Thousand Oaks, CA: Sage Publications, Inc.

Mahoney, A., Wong, S., Pomerleau, J. M., & Pargament, K. I. (2021). Sanctification of diverse aspects of life and psychosocial functioning: A meta-analysis of studies from 1999–2019. *Psychology of Religion & Spirituality*. Advance online publication. https://doi.org/10.1037 /rel0000354

Makris, N., & Pnevmatikos, D. (2007). Children's understanding of human and super-natural mind. *Cognitive Development, 22*(3), 365–75. https://doi.org/10.1016/j.cogdev.2006.12.003

Marks, L. D., & Dollahite, D. C. (2016). *Religion and Families: An Introduction*. New York: Routledge.

Mata-McMahon, J. (2016). Reviewing the research in children's spirituality (2005–2015): Proposing a pluricultural approach. *International Journal of Children's Spirituality, 21*(2), 140–52. https://doi.org/10.1080/1364436X.2016.1186611

McPhail, B. L. (2019). Religious heterogamy and the intergenerational transmission of religion: A cross-national analysis. *Religions, 10*(2), 109. https://doi.org/10.3390/rel10020109

Miller, L. (2015). *The Spiritual Child: The New Science on Parenting for Health and Lifelong Thriving*. New York: St. Martin's Press.

Moodley, T., Esterhuyse, K. G. F., & Beukes, R. B. I. (2012). Factor analysis of the Spiritual Well-Being Questionnaire using a sample of South African adolescents. *Religion and Theology, 19*(1–2), 122–51. https://doi.org/10.1163/157430112X650339

Moore, K., Gomez-Garibello, C., Bosacki, S., & Talwar, V. (2016). Children's spiritual lives: The development of a children's spirituality measure. *Religions, 7*(8), 95. https://doi.org/10.3390/rel7080095

Moore, K., Talwar, V., & Bosacki, S. (2012). Canadian children's perceptions of spirituality: Diverse voices. *International Journal of Children's Spirituality, 7*(3), 217–34. https://doi.org/10.1080/1364436X.2012.742040

Nadal, A. R. C., Hardy, S. A., & Barry, C. M. (2018). Understanding the roles of religiosity and spirituality in emerging adults in the United States. *Psychology of Religion and Spirituality, 10*(1), 30–43. https://doi.org/10.1037/rel0000104

Nelsen, H. M., & Kroliczak, A. (1984). Parental use of the threat "God will punish": Replication and extension. *Journal for the Scientific Study of Religion, 23*(3), 267–77. https://doi.org/10.2307/1386041

Nelson, J. M. (2009). *Psychology, Religion, and Spirituality*. New York: Springer.

Nye, R. (2017). Spirituality as a natural part of childhood. *Bible in Transmission Newsletter.* www.biblesociety.org.uk/content/explore_the_bible/bible_in_transmission/files/2017_spring_v2/transmission_spring_2017_nye.pdf

Nyhof, M. A., & Johnson, C. N. (2017). Is God just a big person? Children's conceptions of God across cultures and religious traditions. *British Journal of Developmental Psychology, 35*(1), 60–75. https://doi.org/10.1111/bjdp.12173

Oman, D. (2013). Defining religion and spirituality. In R. F. Paloutzian & L. Park (eds.), *Handbook of the Psychology of Religion and Spirituality* (2nd ed., pp. 23–47). New York: Guildford Press.

Onedera, J. D. (ed.). (2008). *The Role of Religion in Marriage and Family Counseling.* New York and London: Routledge.

Oulali, I., Bos, H., van den Akker, A., Fukkink, R. G., Merry, M. S., & Overbeek, G. (2019). Development and validation of the Religious Collective Self-Esteem Scale for Children. *Psychology of Religion and Spirituality, 11*(3), 188–202. https://doi.org./10.1037/rel0000145

Ovwigho, P. C., & Cole, A. (2010). Scriptural engagement, communication with God, and moral behavior among children. *International Journal of Children's Spirituality, 15*(2), 101–13. https://doi.org/10.1080/1364436X .2010.497642

Paloutzian, R. F., & Park, C. L. (2021). The psychology of religion and spirituality: How big the tent? *Psychology of Religion and Spirituality, 13* (1), 3–13. https://doi.org/10.1037/rel0000218

Pargament, K. I. (1997). *The Psychology of Religion and Coping: Theory, Research, Practice.* New York: Guilford Press.

Pargament, K. I., Mahoney, A., Exline, J. J., Jones, J. W., & Shafranske, E. (2013). Envisioning an integrative paradigm for the psychology of religion and spirituality: An introduction to the APA handbook of psychology, religion and spirituality. In K. I. Pargament, J. J. Exline, & J. W. Jones (eds.), *APA Handbook of Psychology, Religion, and Spirituality* (vol. 1, pp. 3–19). Washington, DC: American Psychological Association.

Pargament, K. I., & Mahoney, A. (2017). Spirituality: The search for the sacred. In C. R. Snyder, S. J. Lopez, L. M. Edwards, & S. C. Marques (eds.), *The Oxford Handbook of Positive Psychology* (3rd ed.). https://doi.org/10.1093 /oxfordhb/9780199396511.013.51

Pearce, L., & Denton, M. L. (2011). *A Faith of Their Own: Stability and Change in the Religiosity of America's Adolescents.* New York: Oxford University Press.

Pearce, M. J., Little, T. D., & Perez, J. E. (2003). Religiousness and depressive symptoms among adolescents. *Journal of Clinical Child & Adolescent Psychology, 32*(2), 267. https://doi.org/10.1207/S15374424JCCP3202_12

Pearce, L. D., Uecker, J. E., & Denton M. L. (2019). Religion and adolescent outcomes: How and under what conditions religion matters. *Annual Review of Sociology, 45*(1), 201–22. https://doi.org/10.1146/annurev-soc-073117-041317

Pendleton, S. M., Cavalli, K. S., Pargament, K. I., & Nasr, S. Z. (2002). Religious/spiritual coping in childhood cystic fibrosis: A qualitative study. *Pediatrics, 109*(1), 1–11. https://doi.org/10.1542/peds.109.1.e8

Petts, R. J. (2012). Single mothers' religious participation and early childhood behavior. *Journal of Marriage and Family, 74*(2), 251–68. https://doi.org/10.1111/j.1741-3737.2011.00953.x

Petts, R. J., & Kysar-Moon, A. E. (2012). Child discipline and conservative Protestantism: Why the relationship between corporal punishment and child behavior problems may vary by religious context. *Review of Religious Research, 54*(4), 445–68. www.jstor.org/stable/41940803

Pew Research Center (2012, December 18). The global religious landscape. www.pewforum.org/2012/12/18/global-religious-landscape-exec

Pew Research Center (2014, September 18). Families may differ, but they share common values on parenting. www.pewresearch.org/fact-tank/2014/09/18/families-may-differ-but-they-share-common-values-on-parenting

Pew Research Center (2018a, April 25). When Americans say they believe in God, what do they mean? www.pewforum.org/2018/04/25/when-americans-say-they-believe-in-god-what-do-they-mean

Pew Research Center (2018b, June 13). The age gap in religion around the world. www.pewforum.org/2018/06/13/the-age-gap-in-religion-around-the-world

Pew Research Center (2020, September 10). US teens take after their parents religiously, attend services together and enjoy family rituals. www.pewforum.org/2020/09/10/u-s-teens-take-after-their-parents-religiously-attend-services-together-and-enjoy-family-rituals

Rew, L., Wong, Y. J., & Sternglanz, R. (2004). The relationship between prayer, health behaviors, and protective resources in school-aged children. *Issues in Comprehensive Pediatric Nursing, 27*(4), 245–55. https://doi.org/10.1080/01460860490884156

Richert, R. A., Boyatzis, C. J., & King, P. E. (2017). Introduction to the British Journal of Developmental Psychology special issue on religion, culture, and development. *British Journal of Developmental Psychology, 35*(1), 1–3. https://doi.org/10.1111/bjdp.12179

Richert, R. A., & Barrett, J. L. (2005). Do you see what I see? Young children's assumptions about God's perceptual abilities. *International Journal for the Psychology of Religion, 15*(4), 283–95. https://doi.org/10.1207/s15327582ijpr1504_2

Richert, R. A., & Granqvist, P. (2013). Religious and spiritual development in childhood. In R. F. Paloutzian & C. L. Park (eds.), *Handbook of the Psychology of Religion and Spirituality* (pp. 165–82). New York: The Guilford Press.

Richert, R. A., Saide, A. R., Lesage, K. A., & Shaman, N. J. (2017). The role of religious context in children's differentiation between God's mind and human minds. *British Journal of Developmental Psychology, 35*(1), 37–59. https://doi.org/10.1111/bjdp.12160

Richert, R. A., Shaman, N. J., Saide, A. R., & Lesage, K. A. (2016). Folding your hands helps God hear you: Prayer and anthropomorphism in parents and children. *Research in the Social Scientific Study of Religion, 27,* 140–57. https://doi.org/10.1163/9789004322035_010

Richert, R. A., & Smith, E. I. (2009). Cognitive foundations in the development of a religious mind. In E. Voland & W. Schiefenhövel (eds.), *The Biological Evolution of Religious Mind and Behavior* (pp. 181–94). New York: Springer. https://doi.org/443.webvpn.fjmu.edu.cn/10.1007/978-3-642-00128-4_12

Rodriguez, C. M., & Henderson, R. C. (2010). Who spares the rod? Religious orientation, social conformity, and child abuse potential. *Child Abuse & Neglect, 34*(2), 84–94. https://doi.org/10.1016/j.chiabu.2009.07.002

Roehlkepartain, E. C. (2014). Children, religion, and spiritual development: Reframing a research agenda. *The Sage Handbook of Child Research* (pp. 81–99). Thousand Oaks, CA: Sage Publications.

Roehlkepartain, E. C., King, P. E., Wagener, L. M., & Benson, P. L. (eds.) (2006). *The Handbook of Spiritual Development in Childhood and Adolescence.* Thousand Oaks, CA: Sage Publications.

Rostosky, S., Abreu, R. L., Mahoney, A., & Riggle, E. D. B. (2017). A qualitative study of parenting and religion/spirituality in LBGTQ families. *Psychology of Religion and Spirituality, 9*(4), 437–45. https://doi.org/10.1037/rel0000077

Sagberg, S. (2017). Taking a children's rights perspective on children's spirituality. *International Journal of Children's Spirituality, 22*(1), 24–35. https://doi.org/10.1080/1364436X.2016.1276050

Saide, A. R., & Richert, R. A. (2020). Socio-cognitive and cultural influences on children's concepts of God. *Journal of Cognition and Culture, 20*(1–2), 22–40. Advance online publication. https://doi.org/10.1163/15685373-12340072

Santos, C., & Michaels, J. L. (2020). What are the core features and dimensions of "spirituality"? Applying a partial prototype analysis to understand how laypeople mentally represent spirituality as a concept. *Psychology of Religion and Spirituality.* Advance online publication. http://dx.doi./10.1037/rel0000380

Saroglou, V. (2011). Believing, bonding, behaving, and belonging: The big four religious dimensions and cultural variation. *Journal of Cross-Cultural Psychology, 42*(8), 1320–40. https://doi.org/10.1177/0022022111412267

Schleifer, C., & Chaves, M. (2017). Family formation and religious service attendance: Untangling marital and parental effects. *Sociological Methods & Research, 46*(1), 125–52. https://doi.org/10.1177/0049124114526376

Schottenbauer, M. A., Spernak, S. M., & Hellstrom, I. (2007). Relationship between family religious behaviors and child well-being among third-grade children. *Mental Health, Religion and Culture, 10*(2), 191–98. https://doi.org/10.1080/13674670600847394

Shaman, N. J., Saide, A. R., Lesage, K. A., & Richert, R. A. (2016). Who cares if I stand on my head when I pray? Ritual inflexibility and mental-state understanding in preschoolers. *Research in the Social Scientific Study of Religion, 27*, 122–39. https://doi.org/10.1163/9789004322035_009

Shepperd, J. A., Pogge, G., Lipsey, N. P., Miller, W. A., & Webster, G. D. (2019). Belief in a loving versus punitive God and behavior. *Journal of Research on Adolescence, 29*(2), 390–401. https://doi.org/10.1111/jora.12437

Shook, J. R. (2017). Are people born to be believers, or are Gods born to be believed? *Method & Theory in the Study of Religion, 29* (4/5), 353–73. https://doi.org/10.1163/15700682-12341389

Sifers, S. K., Jared, S., Warren, J. S., & Jackson, Y. (2012). Measuring spirituality in children. *Journal of Psychology and Christianity, 31*(3), 209–18.

Silveira, F., Shafer, K., Dufur, M. J., & Roberson, M. (2020). Ethnicity and parental discipline practices: A cross national comparison. *Journal of Marriage and Family*. Advance online publication. https://doi.org/10.1111/jomf.12715

Smith, C. (2017). *Religion: What It Is, How It Works, and Why It Matters*. Princeton, NY: Princeton University Press.

Smith, C., & Adamczyk, A. (2021). *Handing Down the Faith: How Parents Pass Their Religion on to the Next Generation*. New York: Oxford University Press.

Smith, E. I., & Crosby R. G. (2017). Unpacking religious affiliation: Exploring associations between Christian children's religious cultural context, God image, and self-esteem across development. *British Journal of Developmental Psychology, 35*(1), 76–90. https://doi.org/10.1111/bjdp.12156

Smith, C., Ritz, B., & Rotolo, M. (2019). *Religious Parenting: Transmitting Faith and Values in Contemporary America*. Princeton, NY: Princeton University Press.

Spilman, S. K., Neppl, T. K., Donnellan, M. B., Schofield, T. J., & Conger, R. D. (2013). Incorporating religiosity into a developmental model of positive family functioning across generations. *Developmental Psychology, 49*(4), 762–74. https://doi.org/10.1037/a0028418

Starks, B., & Robinson, R. V. (2007). Moral cosmology, religion, and adult values for children. *Journal for the Scientific Study of Religion, 46*(1), 17–35. www.jstor.org/stable/4621950

Stearns, M., & McKinney, C. (2019a). Connection between parent and child religiosity: A meta-analysis examining parent and child gender. *Journal of Family Psychology, 33*(6), 704–10. https://doi.org/10.1037/fam0000550

Stearns, M., & McKinney, C. (2019b). Perceived parent–child religiosity: Moderation by perceived maternal and paternal warmth and autonomy granting and emerging adult gender. *Psychology of Religion and Spirituality, 11*(3), 177–87. https://doi.org/10.1037/rel0000142

Stoyles, G. J., Stanford, B., Caputi, P., Keating, A. L., & Hyde, B. (2012). A measure of spiritual sensitivity for children. *International Journal of Children's Spirituality, 17*(3), 203–15.

Sullivan, S. C. (2011). *Living Faith: Everyday Religion and Mothers in Poverty.* Chicago: University of Chicago Press.

Tamminen, K. (1994). Religious experiences in childhood and adolescence: A viewpoint of religious development between the ages of 7 and 20. *The International Journal for the Psychology of Religion, 4*, 61–85.

Tarakeshwar, N., & Pargament, K. I. (2001). Religious coping in families of children with autism. *Focus on Autism and Other Developmental Disabilities, 16*(4), 247–60. https://doi.org/10.1177/108835760101600408

Thiessen, J., & Wilkins-Laflamme, S. (2020). *None of the Above: Nonreligious Identity in the US and Canada.* New York: New York University Press.

Twenge, J. M., Sherman, R. A., Exline, J. J., & Grubbs, J. B. (2016). Declines in American adults' religious participation and beliefs, 1972–2014. *SAGE Open, 6.* https://doi.org/10.1177/2158244016638133

Uchida, Y., Norasakkunkit, V., & Kitayama, S. (2004). Cultural constructions of happiness: Theory and empirical evidence. *Journal of Happiness Studies, 5*(3), 223–39. https://doi.org/10.1007/s10902-004-8785-9

Uecker, J. E., Mayrl, D., & Stroope, S. (2016). Family formation and returning to institutional religion in young adulthood. *Journal for the Scientific Study of Religion, 55*(2), 384–406. https://doi.org/10.1111/jssr.12271

University of California, Riverside (2020, February 19). $10 million grant will study children's religious views. Press release. https://news.ucr.edu/articles/2020/02/19/10-million-grant-will-study-childrens-religious-views

Van der Jagt-Jelsma, W., de Vries-Schot, M., Scheepers, P., Van Deurzen, P., Klip, H., & Buitelaar, J. (2017). Longitudinal study of religiosity and mental health of adolescents with psychiatric problems: The TRAILS study. *European Psychiatry, 45*, 65–71. https://doi.org/10.1016/j.eurpsy.2017.05.031

Van der Jagt-Jelsma, W., de Vries-Schot, M. R., de Jong, R., Hartman, C. A., Verhulst, F. C., Klip, H., van Deurzen, P. A., & Buitelaar, J. K. (2015). Religiosity and mental health of pre-adolescents with psychiatric problems and their parents: The TRAILS study. *European Psychiatry, 30*(7), 845–51. https://doi.org/10.1016/j.eurpsy.2015.07.006

Van Dyke, C. J., Glenwick, D. S., Cecero, J. J., & Kim, S. (2009). The relationship of religious coping and spirituality to adjustment and psychological distress in urban early adolescents. *Mental Health, Religion & Culture, 12*(4), 369–83. https://doi.org/10.1080/13674670902737723

Voas, D., & Chaves, M. (2016). Is the United States a counterexample to the secularization thesis? *American Journal of Sociology, 121*(5), 1517–56. https://doi.org/10.1086/684202

Weyand, C., O'Laughlin, L., & Bennett, P. (2013). Dimensions of religiousness that influence parenting. *Psychology of Religion and Spirituality, 5*(3), 182–91. https://doi.org/10.1037/a0030627

Whitehead, A. L. (2018). Religion and disability: Variation in religious service attendance rates for children with chronic health conditions. *Journal for the Scientific Study of Religion, 57*(2), 377–95. https://doi.org/10.1111/jssr.12521

WHOQOL Group (1995a). Quality of life assessment: Position paper from the WHO. *Social Science Medicine, 41*, 1403–09.

WHOQOL Group (1995b). Facet definitions and questions. Geneva: Division of Mental Health, WHO. MNH/PSF/95.1.B.

Woolley, J., & Phelps, K. E. (2001). The development of children's beliefs about prayer. *Journal of Cognition and Culture, 1*(2), 139–66. https://doi.org/10.1163/156853701316931380

Yonker, J. E., Schnabelrauch, C. A., & DeHaan, L. G. (2012). The relationship between spirituality and religiosity on psychological outcomes in adolescents and emerging adults: A meta-analytic review. *Journal of Adolescence, 35*(2), 299–314. https://doi.org/10.1016/j.adolescence.2011.08.010

Cambridge Elements ≡

Child Development

Marc H. Bornstein

National Institute of Child Health and Human Development, Bethesda
Institute for Fiscal Studies, London
UNICEF, New York City

Marc H. Bornstein is an Affiliate of the *Eunice Kennedy Shriver* National Institute
of Child Health and Human Development, an International Research Fellow at the
Institute for Fiscal Studies (London), and UNICEF Senior Advisor for Research for ECD
Parenting Programmes. Bornstein is President Emeritus of the Society for Research in Child
Development, Editor Emeritus of *Child Development*, and founding Editor of *Parenting:
Science and Practice.*

About the Series

Child development is a lively and engaging, yet serious and purposeful subject of academic
study that encompasses myriad of theories, methods, substantive areas, and applied
concerns. Cambridge Elements in Child Development proposes to address all these key
areas, with unique, comprehensive, and state-of-the-art treatments, introducing readers
to the primary currents of research and to original perspectives on, or contributions to,
principal issues and domains in the field.

Cambridge Elements ≡

Child Development

Elements in the Series

Printed in the United States
by Baker & Taylor Publisher Services